A Guide to Psychological
Practice in Geriatric
Long-Term Care

THE HAWORTH PRESS
Aging and Gerontology

New, Recent, and Forthcoming Titles:

Long-Term Care Administration: The Management of Institutional and Non-Institutional Components of the Continuum of Care by Ben Abramovice

Psychiatry in the Nursing Home: Assessment, Evaluation, and Intervention by D. Peter Birkett

Women and Aging: Celebrating Ourselves by Ruth Raymond Thone

Victims of Dementia: Services, Support, and Care by Wm. Michael Clemmer

Dietetic Service Operation Handbook: Practical Applications in Geriatric Care by Karen S. Kolasa

A Guide Psychological Practice in Geriatric Long-Term Care by Peter A. Lichtenberg

A Guide
to Psychological
Practice in Geriatric
Long-Term Care

Peter A. Lichtenberg, PhD

The Haworth Press
New York • London • Norwood (Australia)

The Haworth Press, Inc., 10 Alice Street, Binghamton, NY 13904-1580

Library of Congress Cataloging-in-Publication Data

Lichtenberg, Peter A.
   A guide to psychological practice in geriatric long-term care / Peter A. Lichtenberg.
   p. cm.
   Includes bibliographical references and index.
   ISBN 1-56024-410-0 (alk. paper)–156024-411-9 (pbk: alk. paper).
   1. Nursing home patients–Mental health services. 2. Aged–Long-term care–Psychological aspects. 3. Behavior therapy for the aged. I. Title.
   [DNLM: 1. Long-Term Care. 2. Mental Disorders–in old age. 3. Mental Disorders–therapy. 4. Psychotherapy–methods. WT 150 L699g 1993]
RC451.4.N87L53 1993
362.1′6–dc20
DNLM/DLC
for Library of Congress   92-48389
                                                                                    CIP

This book is dedicated to five people: Audrey Turner, Gary Heck, Trina Cook, Sidney Monroe, and Dianna Tolley, who all helped me to find the pure joy of working in geriatric long-term care.

ABOUT THE AUTHOR

Peter A. Lichtenberg, PhD, is Assistant Professor in the School of Medicine at Wayne State University. Previously, he was Assistant Professor at the University of Virginia Medical School and Director of a geriatric long-term care psychology program. Dr. Lichtenberg has completed a post-doctoral fellowship in geriatric neuropsychology and has published twenty professional journal and news articles. He is a member of the Gerontological Society of America, the American Psychological Association, and Psychologists in Long-Term Care.

CONTENTS

Foreword

Even though in aging we have come to equate clinical care with multidisciplinary care, two common situations question the extent of this commitment. Too often, multidisciplinary translates into the dominance of one discipline and the association of others, with (clear or imposed) boundaries delineating hierarchies of responsibilities. Disciplines work in parallel, much like the parallel play of toddlers. Communication serves to maintain the explicit organization and the imposed authority. Alternately, and also too often, boundaries are blurred in an effort to view hierarchies and achieve the (illusion of) equality of disciplines. In this situation disciplines work enmeshed with each other, much like a group of adolescents where the sense of belonging is more important than the achievements. Communication serves to maintain the implicit structure and assumed equality.

True multidisciplinary care is neither vertical, as in the first case, or horizontal, as in the second. It is both and then more–perhaps diagonal. For clinicians of different disciplines–with their respective backgrounds and experiences, modes of thinking and ways of interacting, methods of caring and means of curing–to come together in a stable commitment to the health and quality of life of older adults requires the integration of vertical and horizontal relationships. It entails avowal as well as disavowal of boundaries, not upon the command of others, but at the rational or intuitive encouragement of oneself. It embodies authority, equality, and servitude, not imposed by the structure of people but by the patterns of health and illness, patient and family. It is founded on mutual teaching and learning, that is, the acceptance of and reliance upon the knowledge of others as expanders and catalysts of one's own knowledge. Multidisciplinary care, then, occurs within the polarity of specificity and communality, individuation and collectivity.

Why this attention to multidisciplinary care in the foreword of a book devoted specifically to geriatric psychology? In this book

Peter Lichtenberg calls for psychology to unfold itself into an intellectual and clinical force in the care of older adults. Concurrently, this book invites other disciplines (and certainly my own discipline of nursing) to open themselves up to how psychology can enrich their respective clinical practices and to ponder the integrated geriatric care that may result across, yet in recognition of, disciplinary boundaries.

This book, at its very clinical core, is written with a pragmatic view on elder care that fosters the growth of geriatric psychology while also being intrinsically multidisciplinary. This view de-emphasizes age, illness, and dependence as static indicators of aging and health. Instead, it conceptualizes aging dynamically as a developmental phase with its own challenges, opportunities, and responsibilities; and elder health as attending to quality of life and dignity of death. This view extends beyond the individual patients and includes the patients in interaction with caregivers, family members, and community. In opposition to traditional medical thinking, this view stresses care over cure, with care being a right and cure an infrequent possibility. This view is proactive rather than reactive to the needs and wishes of patients and families, and includes diagnosis and prognosis, treatment and prevention.

The multidisciplinary and pragmatic focus of this book grew out of Dr. Lichtenberg's clinical experiences as a geriatric psychologist "in-the-trenches-and-among-the-troops." These trenches of long-term care were shaped by the people needing care:

- very ill, very frail, and very regressed patients;
- cognitively impaired patients, who can no longer distinguish reality from irreality;
- patients who have lost the sense of person and the sense of interpersonal relationships;
- behaviorally difficult to manage patients, either because of the social intrusiveness of their behavior, or because of the threat they pose to themselves, other patients, or staff;
- patients who have abandoned our world for one that seems incomprehensible and impenetrable; and
- caregivers, many old and frail as well, struggling between commitment and giving up, hope and despair, health and illness.

The troops in these trenches, which have influenced Dr. Lichtenberg's perspectives, have included:

- nursing personnel–professional and paraprofessional, licensed and not-so-licensed, many idling somewhere on the continuum between commitment and indifference;
- physicians of various specialties, many with self-proclaimed rather than self-evident expertise in aging;
- social workers, many of whom saw their clinical creativity blunted by the demands of procedures and regulations;
- many other staff, often confused about their identity as geriatric care providers because of the seeming incompatibility of giving psycho-emotional care to a population with overwhelming physical needs.

This book's organization into two parts enables the reader to gain understanding of both the scope of psychological practice with older adults and of specific applications of psychologcial knowledge and clinical technique with this population. The first part on comprehensive psychological services for the elderly (implicity) presents an integrative model of psychological services as part of geriatric care. The emphasis is not as much on what geriatric psychology has to offer. Rather, by discussing conceptual issues as well as providing practical advice, Dr. Lichtenberg shows how geriatric psychology and other geriatric disciplines can blend into a diversified and rich clinical environment for caring for older adults. The chapters on neuropsychology first sketch the role of the neuropsychologist, not just the traditional role of a diagnostician, but also the dynamic team role of interpreter, educator, and intervention strategist. The chapter on neuropsychological test batteries orients both the users of test batteries (psychologists) and the users of test results (clinicians from other disciplines) to various assessment schedules, highlighting information and strategies relevant to both groups of clinicians. The chapter on team building highlights how psychological science can be applied to enhance clinical learning by paraprofessional nursing (and other) staff, and to improve team functioning. This chapter and the one on paraprofessionals are good examples of the sense of reality that Dr. Lichtenberg brings to the book. Too often, books (platonically) emphasize the ideal or near-ideal world of how things

xii PSYCHOLOGICAL PRACTICE IN GERIATRIC LONG-TERM CARE

should be in long-term care, claiming along the way that thinking at the levels of ideas and ideals will trickle down into more realistic applications.

The second part of the book focuses on pertinent and often ignored clinical issues. This part gently prods psychologists to use their theoretical background and clinical training to explore new foci of care. Alcohol abuse, largely unrecognized and untreated in the elderly, is highly prevalent among geropsychiatric patients. Debunking some common myths, Dr. Lichtenberg sensitizes us to the need for clinical attention to alcohol abuse and describes realistic approaches to incorporating a clinical focus on alcoholism into geriatric care. Sexuality in older adults and dementia patients in particular, another issue long ignored in geriatric care, distinguishes normal from abnormal sexual behavior. Dr. Lichtenberg wonderfully puts the reader at ease about the inevitable uncomfortableness that comes with discussing geriatric sexuality. This, in turn, enables the reader to develop a sensitive and pragmatic understanding of issues, problems, and approaches. Another area in geriatric care that has been held back by myths and misconceptions is that of older adults' benefit from psychotherapeutic intervention. In a related chapter, we learn how to adapt traditional methods of psychotherapy to use with various groups of older adults. The reader is also confronted with the need to adapt him- or herself as a geriatric psychotherapist—perhaps just as important a clinical strategy! The second part of the book closes with a chapter on caregivers. Even though the caregiving literature has grown immensely in the last decade or so, the field of aging seems to have difficulty extricating itself from description of problems and issues facing caregivers, and to systematically and comprehensively address how we can help caregivers. The final chapter takes a bold step in the latter direction.

The multidisciplinary perspective that permeates this book opens up the emerging field of geriatric psychology to other disciplines, giving them an opportunity to explore what they can receive from geriatric psychology practice, but also what they can give to it. Both psychologists and nonpsychologists will find this book to be an *invitation* to geriatric psychology, its unique perspectives and contributions, and its interdependence with other disciplines. In its encouraging and hopeful tone, this book brings to geriatric care a renewed recognition that change can be effected in older adults' behavior, emotion, cognition, and personality. It stresses growth and health, but within a realistic context of decline and illness. It reaffirms to such disciplines as nursing, social work, and medicine that their practice is based in part on central principles of psychological science, such as, for instance, development, interpersonal and intrapersonal dynamics, and social environment. It also reclaims from these disciplines some of the naive uses or outright misapplications of this knowledge.

Ivo L. Abraham, PhD, RN
Associate Professor of Nursing
Associate Professor of Behavioral Medicine and Psychiatry
Director, Center on Aging and Health
Co-Director, Southeastern Rural Mental Health Research Center
University of Virginia

Acknowledgements

It has been my good fortune to have been hired by two renowned psychologists, Jeffrey Barth, PhD, and Mitchell Rosenthal, PhD. They have not only helped me to improve my skills but have also been true mentors. Their guidance and support directly led to this book. I am also indebted to several colleagues who helped to create the programs and practices described here and who made editorial comments on earlier versions of this work: Drs. Debby Strzepek, Carol Manning, Bernice Marcopulos, and Carol McLain. Drs. Ann Gibbons, Bob Guenther, and Louis Burgio also provided me with excellent assistance. I am indebted to Michael Nanna for his tremendous help. Finally, I thank all of the professionals whose work I drew from–it has been inspirational to become well acquainted with so much fine work in gerontology. I also thank Mr. Lyn Harding and his staff at Western State Hospital in Staunton, Virginia.

I have enjoyed tremendous love and support from my wife, Katherine. Katherine helped me with this project from its inception. My extended family (Erik, Andy, Debby and Tom Lichtenberg, Carol Mermey, Herb and Ann McMullen, and Peggy Delmore) have all provided me with encouragement and enthusiasm. My parents, Philip and Elsa Lichtenberg, have my appreciation for their lifelong love and friendship.

Chapter 1

Introduction

It has only been in the last 15 years that psychologists have been viewed as valuable service providers in geriatric long-term-care settings. Hyerstay (1979) described the varied roles of change agent, advocate, therapist, family and staff educator, trainer, and researcher as befitting psychologists. In the 1970s, nursing homes replaced state mental hospitals as the major receiving site for mentally ill elderly, thus creating the need for psychological assessments and interventions with patients who demonstrate disorientation, depression, and agitation (Smyer, 1986). As more nursing homes dealt with the geriatric mentally ill, there was also a growing need for psychological intervention with long-term-care staff and relatives of patients.

The largest increase in geropsychological practice has been in the area of behavioral consultation. MacDonald (1983) pointed out that since initial staff and administrative expectations of psychologists are so unrealistic, psychologists need to develop four features in their consulting practice. First, there must be nontoken administrative support. Administrative staff decide who gets to spend time with the consultant, and they can provide support for the new emphasis on mental health. Second, there needs to be a collaborative relationship established with the facility medical personnel. Third, the consultant should have expertise in general geriatric psychiatry as well as in behavior therapy. This is necessary so he or she does not fall victim to certain ageist ideas that hold that most older adults dwell in long-term care facilities or that dementia is an inevitable condition of aging. Finally, there must be regular staff meetings that focus solely on improving psychological care. It is in the staff meetings that the consultant can illustrate the relationship between residents' behavior and the environmental contingencies.

There has been tremendous success in enhancing prosocial behaviors and reducing problem behaviors through behavioral treatment. Sanavio (1981) highlighted his toilet retraining program that was based on work by Azrin and Foxx (1971). To increase the frequency of urination, the patient was given large quantities of his or her favorite drink and snack each hour. The trainer then guided the patient to the bathroom. The patient stayed on the toilet for five minutes; if successful voiding occurred, he or she was presented with verbal praise and a small reinforcer. A urine alarm assessed wetting accidents and led to an overcorrection procedure by the patient. Using an A-B-A design, Sanavio demonstrated success in eliminating incontinence in an elderly man.

Block et al. (1987) focused their consultation on the difficult patients whose problems most frustrated the staff. After a one-hour introductory session on behavioral principles, two residents were selected for behavioral treatment. Antecedents and consequences to problem behaviors were specified. The nursing aides then identified reinforcers and started an intervention. Ongoing feedback was presented to the staff by the consultant. This method helped to increase dressing behavior in one patient and to reduce combative behavior in another.

Hussian and Davis (1985) presented behavioral interventions that were applied to a number of problems faced by geriatric long-term-care patients. Increasing patient ambulation, decreasing incontinence, and increasing grooming skills were but a few of the topics addressed. They made use of extensive behavioral chains (e.g., a chain for shaving was composed of 13 steps) and positive reinforcement. The Premack Principle and Differential Reinforcement of Other Behavior (DRO) were other behavioral plans that they found to be successful.

While behavioral consultation has enormous benefits, it does not eliminate the need for other psychological services. In behaviorally treating incontinence, for example, emotional reactions to stroke can be neglected. Aging and relocating to a long-term-care facility is known to be associated with issues of loss. Grief, depression, and interpersonal conflicts are examples of problems less likely to be addressed by consultants. Traditional services–such as psychotherapy with long-term-care patients and/or their family caregivers–have been shown to be effective, but they are underutilized (Thompson et al., 1986). Less traditional services–such as alcohol-abuse detection and treatment, and therapy for sexual dysfunction–are often needed by elderly patients. In addition, the recent growth in Geriatric Neuropsychology provides new ways of understanding and intervening in patient problems. To date, however, there are no descriptions of actual programs that deliver comprehensive services to long-term-care patients. Thus, the elderly continue to be underserved.

It was my early professional experience in long-term care that drove home to me how neglected our elderly remain and how few written resources we have to teach us about this population. Upon starting as the only psychologist for a 180-bed long-term-care setting, I organized a consultation service. As a result, my staff alerted me to the more serious behavioral problems. One of my first referrals was to evaluate a man who was "throwing himself to the floor due to manipulative tendencies." Upon interviewing the staff, it was clear that this man was perceived as falling just to obtain staff attention. A one-day baseline observation period was performed, and we were astounded to note that he fell 31 times. My observations and interviews of this patient indicated that he often slumped to the floor without warning, often losing his balance. In addition, he had severe verbal communication difficulties, was frequently tearful, had stopped eating, and was losing a considerable amount of weight. In the following months, this patient received comprehensive assessments and treatments. (A neurologist diagnosed that his falls were caused by Parkinson's disease.) Speech therapy enabled the patient to use a Voc-aid, which greatly improved his communication skills, and the psychology staff provided counseling and a behavior program to increase his social interactions. His depression remitted, and he began to function at a higher level than he had in years.

Another of my early consultations was to "help quiet a man who yelled frequently." Upon performing my consultation, I met this yeller, a graduate of the University of Chicago who had suffered from long-term paranoid ideation. In addition, he had become diabetic, had had a below-the-knee amputation, and was rapidly becoming blind. He had previously been in a nursing home that neglected his diabetes, and he had entered a coma. Because of his tremendous vocabulary and history of education, the staff believed that he "knew better" than to yell. Observations indicated that this man sat alone in his room most of the day, while his calls for help were ignored. A neuropsychological assessment revealed that although he performed well on over-learned verbal material, he had many cognitive deficits in attention, memory, visuospatial abilities, and abstract reasoning. Once again, a comprehensive plan including increased activity services, medical monitoring, and counseling served to improve this man's condition.

Addressing the concerns of these two patients was often a frustrating and frightening process. There was very little literature to guide me. And while behavioral techniques were helpful, they did not address the widespread problems that I encountered. It was at this point that the idea for a practical book on delivering geropsychological service was developed. My years of experience with difficult problems and concerns have been ones of constant challenge, out of which evolved a comprehensive approach to geropsychological care.

I learned quickly that the patient problems were only one part of the challenges in long-term care. It was astounding and intimidating to watch the communication patterns among staff. The main rule, though not written anywhere, was clear: If you were a nursing assistant, a licensed practical nurse, or an activities aide, you did not speak to a doctor or supervisor unless given permission. As with most long-term-care facilities, the assistants who provide most of the care were not even allowed to attend treatment-team meetings. They were also very wary of talking to patients about anything emotional or serious. One assistant who was comforting a patient just diagnosed with cancer was told not to "depress the patient" by allowing him to grieve. "Cheer him up instead," the assistant was advised. It did not take long to see that the lonely and neglected patients were served by a staff that was equally lonely and neglected. Comprehensive care for the elderly should be delivered by a responsive, interdisciplinary team. The goal of this book is to provide the means by which our elderly citizens can receive care that empowers them, builds their self-esteem, and does not leave them as shut-ins waiting to die. To do this, new and creative comprehensive approaches must be used. These approaches must train and empower all staff to be a part of the treatment and not to withdraw in fear and ignorance.

This book will be divided into two major parts. In the first part, a comprehensive program of psychological services will be described. This program is based on: (1) incorporating neuropsychology into long-term-care treatment; (2) developing a successful interdisciplinary approach; and (3) creating trained paraprofessional roles to support mental-health services. Throughout this section, pertinent literature in each of these areas will be carefully reviewed, and the new ideas presented on psychological programming will be illustrated by case vignettes.

In the second part of the book, the focus will be on special clinical topics. These will include alcohol abuse, psychotherapy, sexuality, and caregiver issues. Each of these areas has a literature in clinical gerontology, but their applications to long-term care are sparse. Literature reviews will also be followed by case examples. This book will hopefully serve as a guide for the practitioner in long-term care. As such, assessment tools and intervention techniques will be described and highlighted.

REFERENCES

Azrin, N., and Foxx, R. (1971). A Rapid Method of Toilet Training the Institutionalized Retarded. *Journal of Applied Behavior Analysis, 4*, 89-99.

Block, C., Boczkowski, J., Hansen, N., and Vanderbeck, M. (1987). Nursing Home Consultation: Difficult Residents and Frustrated Staff. *The Gerontologist, 27*, 443-446.

Hyerstay, B. (1979). The Role of a Psychologist in a Nursing Home. *Professional Psychology, 10*, 36-41.

Hussian, R., and Davis, R. (1985). *Responsive Care: Behavioral Interventions with Elderly Persons*. Research Press: Illinois.

MacDonald, M. (1983). Behavioral Consultation in Geriatric Settings. *The Behavior Therapist, 6*, 172-174.

Sanavio, E. (1981). Toilet Training Psychogeriatric Residents. *Behavior Modification, 5*, 417-427.

Smyer, M. (1986). Providing Psychological Services in Nursing Homes. *The Clinical Psychologist*, 105-108.

Thompson, L., Davies, R., Gallagher, D., and Krantz, S. (1986). Cognitive Therapy with Older Adults. *Clinical Gerontologist, 5*, 245-278.

Chapter 2

Introducing Neuropsychology
to Geriatric Long-Term Care

Most elderly patients in long-term care suffer from some degree of cognitive impairment (Smyer, 1986). Because of this, neuropsychological assessment, the study of brain-behavior relationships, can be an extremely useful component of long-term care. Clinical neuropsychology is the application of brain-behavior knowledge to patients. Clinical neuropsychology is a subspecialty within clinical psychology, and it has rapidly expanded since the early 1970s. Currently, neuropsychologists complete their doctorate in psychology, and then spend one to two years in post-doctoral training obtaining advanced supervised experience in neuropsychology. At this stage, students learn about the variety of ways neuropsychology can be used with geriatric long-term-care patients. (In the following chapter, specific neuropsychological tests and testing methods will be described and case examples discussed.) The best way to describe neuropsychology is to discuss the roles of a neuropsychologist and to review common referral questions asked of neuropsychologists.

ROLES OF THE NEUROPSYCHOLOGIST
IN LONG-TERM CARE

The neuropsychologist should function in the following roles in long-term care:

- Interpreter
- Educator
- Diagnostician
- Intervention strategist

The neuropsychologist serves as an interpreter of documented information about brain-behavior relationships. Many long-term-care patients have had careful medical examinations that have revealed cerebral damage; such damage has left these patients unable to care for themselves. This information, usually conveyed in highly technical reports, can be summarized by the neuropsychologist so that all staff can understand the information. Even most neuropsychological assessment reports contain considerable jargon, and are only useful if someone can interpret them to the entire staff.

The neuropsychologist also functions in the ongoing role of educator. In Lichtenberg, Marcopulos, McLain, Manning and Sautter (1992), a case was described in which neuropsychological deficits accounted for behavior that staff had viewed as somatic delusions. Rather than viewing this patient as suffering from insanity with hallucinations, the staff began to appreciate his brain impairment. Similarly, an intellectually brilliant patient, now suffering dementia, confused the staff because although he was able to converse in a sophisticated manner, he was nevertheless unable to perform his Activities of Daily Living (ADLs) or remember his daily schedule. The staff thought the man was simply being stubborn and obstinate. A comprehensive evaluation indicated severe frontal lobe damage. Thus he could access his conversational skills, but could not organize his activities, nor keep his schedule straight (Lichtenberg, Heck, and Turner, 1988). Once this was demonstrated, the staff reformulated their expectations of him.

The neuropsychologist often assumes the role of a diagnostician. It is important to remember the limitations of neuropsychology as well as its strengths. Specific brain lesions are best detected by neuroradiological techniques (CT scan, MRI scan), not by neuropsychological testing. Secondly, dementia is often exacerbated by medical problems that need to be treated by Geriatricians and geriatric nurses. That said, the neuropsychologist is often in a good position to integrate information and provide diagnostic input.

The most important role of a neuropsychologist in long-term care is to help create and implement interventions. Neuropsychological data must be tied to practical approaches for enhancing the capabilities of the long-term-care patient and for providing methods for reducing patients' problems. A hypothesis testing model is recommended whereby a plan of intervention is chosen and then, when implemented, is evaluated quantitatively. If the plan is not working, it should be modified. In summary, neuropsychologists can, and should, function in a variety of roles in the long-term-care setting. Neuropsychology is a powerful addition to any clinical program of long-term care.

COMMON NEUROPSYCHOLOGICAL REFERRALS

Geriatric Neuropsychology–the study of brain-behavior relationships to determine if brain impairment exists–became an important field in the 1980s because of its utility in identifying cognitive decline, a core symptom of dementia. Indeed, a work group on the diagnosis of Alzheimer's disease, which was established by the National Institute of Neurologic and Communicative Disorders and Stroke (NINCDS) (McKhann et al., 1984), elevated the role of Geriatric Neuropsychology. The diagnostic criteria created by the NINCDS for probable Alzheimer's disease included evidence of intellectual decline determined by neuropsychological testing. In the early 1980s, leading neuropsychologists were also beginning to highlight problems particular to the elderly (Lezak, 1983; Wedding et al., 1986). As interest in Geriatric Neuropsychology grew, comprehensive books related to the topic were produced (Albert and Moss, 1988; Hunt and Lindley, 1989).

The most frequent referral questions encountered by a neuropsychologist in long-term care are: (1) Is the patient demented? (2) Is the patient depressed? or (3) Is the patient depressed and/or demented? Knowing basic clinical characteristics and using assessment instruments can be extremely useful in answering these questions.

Is the Patient Demented?

Dementia is defined as a loss of cognitive abilities of sufficient severity so as to interfere with social or occupational functioning (*Diagnostic and Statistical Manual* [DSM] III-R). Although there have been over 100 documented causes of dementia, the most common ones found in geriatric long-term care are:

- Alzheimer's disease
- Multi-Infarct Dementia
- Dementia caused by alcohol abuse
- Stroke
- Medication
- Infection

Albert (1988) identified assessments for dementia as attempts to measure functioning in five cognitive domains: attention, language, memory, visuospatial ability, and abstract reasoning. Albert (1988) described attention as including three aspects: (1) orienting to important stimuli (focusing attention); (2) blocking out extraneous stimuli (selective attention); and (3) continuing to concentrate on the stimuli (sustained attention). Attention is the basic cognitive function necessary for the higher-level cognitions (e.g., memory, abstract reasoning) and for task completion. In long-term care, attentional deficits can impair dressing, feeding, participation in activities, and even communication. While changing into pajamas to go to sleep, for example, one of the long-term-care patients would inevitably begin the process smoothly, only to become enamored by an object across the room halfway through changing. He and the nursing assistants would engage in a nightly tug of war because he was not able to sustain attention. This was corrected when the lights were dimmed to provide a calmer environment and the patient was prompted with a series of ongoing one-step commands to help him maintain his focus.

Strub and Black (1985) stressed that since language is the basic means of human communication, it must be tested early on in the assessment. Aphasia, a true language disturbance, can present in many ways. In an expressive aphasia, the output of speech is drastically reduced, and the words are often incomprehensible. The aphasic patient's understanding of language in this case is generally better than their expression of language. Damage to the portion of the brain surrounding Broca's area, a part of the brain in the left frontal region, is associated with expressive aphasia. In receptive aphasia, the comprehension of speech is drastically reduced; and while intelligible sounds are put forth by the aphasic, they are often nonsensical.

A case of receptive aphasia was discovered in a patient whom no one suspected of having a language disorder. She was an 85-year-old, sweet-looking woman who smiled whenever anyone approached her. After being approached, she would say, "I am fine; how are you?" She was generally quiet, but always congenial. When I tried to hold a more in-depth conversation, she began to spew forth nonsense words. This woman had concealed her impairment by displaying highly developed social graces and by being able to "read" the situation, though not comprehending the language around her. Receptive aphasia has long been associated with Wernicke's area, a portion of the left posterior cerebral hemisphere. Other portions of language that need to be assessed include naming (objects, colors, etc.), repetition, reading, writing, and spelling. Many times, aphasic symptoms include both receptive and expressive deficits as well as other communication problems. Language is the principal means by which we communicate; if impaired, communication goals must become a priority of treatment.

Memory disturbances represent the most common initial complaint in Geriatric Neuropsychology. Memory includes the storage and recall of perceptions and experiences (Albert, 1988; Strub and Black, 1985). Primary memory refers to the immediate recall of information, whereas secondary memory refers to delayed recall. Primary memory is not thought to change much with age, but secondary memory is known to decline with normal aging. Age decrements are shown to be greater on recall versus recognition memory tasks (Erber, 1974; Howell, 1972). Severe memory problems are prominent symptoms of Alzheimer's disease and many other forms of dementia (and memory complaints frequently accompany depression and anxiety). Memory testing in geriatric patients should include immediate and delayed recall of verbal and visuospatial information as well as recognition tasks. It is important to work with instruments that have some data on elderly individuals, or else test results may be impossible to interpret.

Memory disturbances can have dramatic effects on long-term-care residents. Ten minutes following the receipt of her pain medication, a memory-impaired patient would demand her medication, working herself into a tantrum when it was refused. By making a medication board on which the patient placed a pin in the appropriate box when given her medication, her nightly tantrum was eliminated. Long-term-care residents must often learn such new skills as wheelchair mobility, safety precautions, and transfer techniques; memory disturbance can heighten the risk of injuries related to carrying out these new skills.

Visuospatial skills refer to motor and perceptual abilities that do not readily lend themselves to verbalization (Lezak, 1983). This includes processing and storing visual information, visual recognition, copying, and visuomotor tracking. The Block Design subtest of the Wechsler Adult Intelligence Scale-Revised (WAIS-R) is a commonly used three-dimensional test of visuoconstructional abilities. Performance on such complex visuospatial tasks declines with normal aging, although much of the decline may be due to slowed response time (Albert, 1988). Simple copying of two-dimensional drawings (e.g., a clock or cross) are typically included in evaluating visuospatial skills.

Abstract reasoning refers to the ability to form mental sets and to demonstrate mental flexibility. An example of a test often used to measure abstract reasoning is the Similarities subtest on the WAISR, in which the task is to explain the similarity between two different objects or situations (e.g., apple-banana; poem-statue). Explaining proverbs or shifting cognitive sets, as in the Wisconsin Card Sorting Test, are other tests of abstract reasoning.

The diagnostic evaluation for dementia consists of two phases. First, identifying the syndrome (i.e., establishing that dementia exists). Second, determining the cause(s) (Strub and Black, 1985). Cognitive testing is employed to identify the syndrome and to determine if the impairment is generalized or specific to one brain area.

The identification of dementia during the neuropsychological evaluation is guided by the following questions:

1. *Is there evidence of cerebral impairment?* Results from the assessment instruments must be compared with normative data (which can often be lacking) and interpreted within the context of a person's educational, occupational, medical, and psychosocial history. In addition, the neuropsychologist must be wary of any psychiatric disorders in the patient (e.g., depression or anxiety) that may cause impaired test results (Jenike, 1988; Marcopulos, 1989).

New and exciting research efforts aimed at improving norms and assessment instruments are underway. Does the evaluation yield behavioral data (most often these are test results) that signifies brain damage? The neuropsychologist compares the patient's test scores with those from normal (non-demented) elderly who share similar educational and vocational histories. The importance of this approach was illustrated when a student, testing an 80-year-old man, reported that the man's memory was severely impaired. She had based this conclusion on his memory subtest score. As her comparison score for the test results of the 80-year old, the student had applied the scores within the average range for a 30-year old. As was reviewed earlier, memory declines occur in normal aging and, thus, scores within the average range for an 80-year old were significantly less than that for a 30-year old. Looking at the scores from this viewpoint, it was concluded that the man's memory score was normal for his age.

2. *What areas of cognition are most affected?* Once brain impairment is noted, it is prudent to begin examining cognitive strengths and weaknesses. To do so, one typically reviews test scores and behavioral evidence in all five areas of cognition and then decides whether these areas are intact or are mildly, moderately, or severely impaired. Neuropsychological assessment can be very useful in describing specific cognitive strengths and weaknesses. For example, a patient with multi-infarct dementia may have a different neuropsychological profile than a patient with Alzheimer's disease. Even among patients diagnosed with Alzheimer's disease, there are differences. Martin et al. (1986) reported that there can be two different "types" of Alzheimer patients—one having language deficits and one having visuospatial deficits. It is necessary to tie together the areas of cognition because certain areas of strength may compensate for other areas of weakness. For example, a hospitalized 89-year-old widow who had no family in the area was evaluated. She was having grave problems walking due to swelling in her legs. On the neuropsychology exam, mild-to-moderate memory difficulties were noted. Thus, the question arose, can this woman return to her apartment or does she need to enter a long-term-care facility?

Upon reviewing the neuropsychology results further, and by follow-up questioning, new insights were discovered: the patient had excellent attentional skills and intact abstract reasoning. She used these skills to compensate for her memory problems. For example, she marked off her calendar each time she took her prescribed medicines, thus avoiding confusion and eliminating the risk of overmedicating herself. A home call revealed several more compensatory strategies, and it was decided that she could safely return home.

A well-detailed description of cognitive strengths and weaknesses provides important information regarding how the patient can best function. This information can help to answer the following: How can this individual best learn new skills or information, or best retain what they currently know? What modalities are the best for communication (verbal vs. visual)? What cognitive strengths can best be used in leisure or social activities? How will the cognitive deficits affect ADL skills?

3. *How are the test results tied to practical recommendations?* Since neuropsychology began as an aid to diagnosis, practical applications of test results have lagged behind. Recommendations must be practical, however, if the testing is to be useful in long-term care. One moderately demented patient was noted to be extremely slow in processing information during the testing. This same man was often physically assaultive to the staff during morning care. It was recommended that delivery of his morning care be paced more slowly so that he could comprehend what was happening. The nursing staff implemented this by turning on the light and saying good morning to the patient ten minutes before they came back to dress him. By that time, he was calm and ready to dress. Another practical recommendation was utilized in a man who became agitated when asked open-ended questions (e.g., "What did you have for lunch?") that he could not answer adequately due to memory problems. Yet his recognition memory was far superior to his recall of material. When given a forced-choice question ("Did you have ham or turkey for lunch?"), he usually responded correctly and did not become agitated. Neuropsychological testing can also grade severity and rate of progression. Neuropsychologists can dissemi-

nate this information to direct-care staff to help explain patients' behaviors and to guide intervention strategies. Neuropsychologists can also help staff recognize treatable causes of cognitive impairment such as anxiety or depression.

Is the Patient Depressed?

Depression in the physically ill elderly is a common problem in long-term care, but, tragically, one that is most often overlooked and misunderstood. Two large epidemiological studies in community elderly revealed that major depression is rare in community elders, compared with medically ill and institutionalized elderly (Blazer, Hughes, and George, 1987; Kramer et al., 1985). In a survey of over 3,000 cases, the Kramer group reported that 0.7% of those age 65-74 suffered from major depression and 1.3% of those age 75 and over suffered from major depression. Blazer, Hughes, and George (1987) reported very similar results with regard to major depressive illness. In light of these findings in the community elderly, it is alarming to find that 20 years of research has consistently documented that elderly medical outpatients and inpatients have depression rates ranging from 15%-45% (Kitchell et al., 1982; Norris et al., 1987; Okimoto et al., 1982; Rapp, Parisi, and Walsh, 1988; Schuckit, Miller, and Hahlbohm, 1975; and Waxman and Carner, 1984), making it at least 12 times more likely in this group. There was only one study that investigated depression in cognitively intact, physically impaired elderly in long-term care (Parmelee, Katz, and Lawton, 1989). They found that 20% of new admissions and 42% of longer-term residents suffered from either major or minor depression. These results are entirely consistent with the studies mentioned above.

Several points must be kept in mind when interpreting these studies, however. All but one of the studies was conducted on a male veteran population; the one study that included a sizeable sample of women did not look at differential rates of depression based on sex. Secondly, it was only in the Rapp, Parisi, and Walsh study (1988) that the reliability and validity of the diagnostic interview results were assessed. Nevertheless, even with these shortcomings the studies raise the following questions: (1) How well is depression assessed by non-psychiatric physicians? (2) Can diagnostic accuracy in primary physicians be improved? (3) What is the most practical method of assessing depression? and (4) What are the consequences of depression?

Depression in medically ill patients of all ages has consistently been underrecognized by primary physicians, particularly with the elderly medical patient. In a sample of 96 family-medicine outpatients, physicians accurately detected only 22% of existing depression (Moore, Silimperi, and Bobula, 1978). Nielsen and Williams (1980) reported that in a sample of 526 outpatients, only 10% were correctly diagnosed with depression, although 50% were noted to have some psychopathology. Waxman and Carner (1984) and Rapp et al. (1988) reported on samples involving only elderly, medically ill patients. Their results were similar to one another and are stunning. In the Waxman and Carner study, physicians correctly identified only 11% of those who were depressed. In the Rapp study, only 8.7% of depressed patients were correctly identified by the primary physician.

These data return us to the second question raised earlier: Can primary physicians' diagnostic accuracy be improved? Research in this area has been encouraging. In three studies, subjects of general medical practices completed screening measures for their level of depression. The results from half of the group were shared with the primary physician, while results from the other half were kept secret. Detection rates of depression were then calculated (German et al., 1987; Linn and Yager, 1980; and Moore, Silimperi, and Bobula, 1978). The results were impressive. In the Moore study, depression was noted 22% of the time in the group without the screening information and 56% of the time when the physicians did receive the screening measure results. Linn and Yager found that detection of depression was three times greater in the physician group receiving the screening results, versus the physicians without the screening information. German et al. (1987) was the largest study by far (N = 1,242), and it was the only one specifically focused on older medical patients. They reported a significantly greater rate of detection in the group receiving feedback (63% vs. 41%).

Are screening measures, then, the most economical and accurate way of detecting depression? One decade of research points exactly to this conclusion. Rapp and Davis (1989) found that even when physicians believe depression to be prevalent in the older population, only a handful routinely ask any questions in their evaluation regarding depressive symptoms. Two self-reporting depression-screening instruments—the Beck Depression Inventory (Nielsen and Williams, 1980) and Zung Self-Rating Depression Scale (Kitchell et al., 1982; Okimoto et al., 1982)—were found to have good sensitivity and specificity scores for the elderly. Sensitivity refers to the ability of the screening measure to detect truly depressed patients (i.e., the concordance between screening measure categorization, depressed/non-depressed, and the physician diagnosis). Specificity refers to the ability of the screening measure to detect truly non-depressed patients. In the later 1980s, with the creation of the Geriatric Depression Scale, two studies compared screening measures (Norris et al., 1987; Rapp, Parisi, and Walsh, 1988). It was concluded in both studies that the Geriatric Depression Scale had the best combined sensitivity and specificity scores: Sensitivity was 0.89 and 0.70, whereas specificity was 0.83 and 0.92.

In this discussion, depression has been identified as an underrecognized problem. Feedback to primary physicians via screening measures reduces the rate of hidden depression. Attention is now turned to the least discussed (but perhaps most potent) issue: What are the consequences of depression? Only one of the studies cited in this chapter attempted to answer this question. Rapp, Parisi, and Walsh (1988) found that compared with non-depressed controls and patients who were not depressed but had other psychiatric problems, depressed patients had the poorest health status. They had significantly more sick days, poorer overall health, and greater functional impairment.

A second consequence of depression is cognitive impairment (Gibson, 1981; LaRue et al., 1986; LaRue, 1989; Weingartner et al., 1981; and Williams et al., 1987). Although the studies consistently revealed memory loss, the nature of the deficit was debated. Weingartner et al. (1981) compared depressed inpatients with normals (mean age of 44) on recall trials of various word lists. The authors concluded that memory impairments were found only when depressed subjects were given words randomly assigned together, but not when the words had contextual meaning. When a list of 12 words from four categories (contextual cues) were presented to a slightly older depressive group, however, their performance was significantly poorer than the normal group (Williams et al., 1987). This result did not support Weingartner's argument (i.e., that deficits are seen only when memory requires effortful processing).

The nature of memory impairment in the depressed elderly is also equivocal. Gibson (1981) found that in comparing demented, depressed, and normal subjects on word-list and line-drawing recall, the depressed group scored significantly better than the demented group and significantly worse than normals. An in-depth analysis revealed that like normals, depressed patients showed both a primacy and recency effect (i.e., they learned words from the beginning and end of the list better than the middle). The demented subjects showed only a recency effect.

LaRue and her colleagues studied memory functions in elderly depressed individuals by utilizing test instruments that are used in neuropsychological practice. In the first set of studies, they evaluated the diagnostic utility of these clinical tests of memory with depressed, demented, and normal subjects. Only Fuld's Object Memory Exam discriminated between the three groups. In a cross-validation effort of 18 Alzheimer's and seven depressed patients, 83% of the Alzheimer's and 85% of the depressed patients were correctly identified by scores on the Object Memory Exam. LaRue (1989) furthered this area of study by including three groups (an Alzheimer's group, a depressed group, and a second demented–non-Alzheimer's–group). Whereas the depressed group scored significantly better than the Alzheimer's group, they did not score differently than the other dementia group. In addition, there were no unique learning patterns among any of the groups. Memory impairment, then, has been consistently found in depressed elderly patients. Distinguishing between depression and dementia on the basis of memory scores is difficult.

Is the Patient Depressed or Is He/She Demented?

Research findings in the last decade have clarified the relationship between dementia and depression. Early in the 1980s there was hope that many elderly who seemed to be stricken with dementia were in fact suffering from a curable depressive pseudodementia (Wells, 1979). In his seminal paper, Wells reviewed the clinical characteristics of patients with depressive pseudodementia versus those of truly demented patients (see Table 2.1).

Pseudodementia patients typically have a more rapid onset of symptoms and are extremely concerned about their cognitive problems, emphasizing their disabilities. In contrast, dementia patients typically have a slow onset of symptoms. Behaviorally, they often go to great lengths to conceal any disability and to avoid seeing a health-care professional (Chenoweth and Spencer, 1986).

Throughout the last ten years, researchers across the world have found that in both outpatient and inpatient populations, depression with dementia was four times more common than was pseudodementia (McLean, 1987; Reifler and Larson, 1989). Reifler and Larson reviewed their first 200 cases since they opened the first Alzheimer's clinic in the early 1980s. Instead of numerous pseudodementia patients, these authors discovered excess disability in patients whose impairments were greater than was warranted by the dementing illness. Twenty-four percent of the patients had depression as a secondary problem. When treated with anti-depressant medication, most of these patients improved their self-care. LaRue (1989) found lower memory scores in both the depressed Alzheimer's patients and in the depressed other-dementia patients (compared with the non-depressed in their respective groups).

Research at other Alzheimer's and long-term-care centers have consistently found a high prevalence of depression and dementia. Seventeen percent of 144 consecutive outpatient admissions had a major depression in a study by Rovner et al. (1989). Ten percent of demented long-term-care patients had major depression, and another 14% had minor depression (Parmelee, Katz, and Lawton, 1989); 11% of 232 demented inpatients had a major depression (Greenwald et al., 1989). The question that arises from these results is, given the prevalence of depression and dementia, how is the depression to be identified? Is it to be based solely on a professional observer's judgment? Or can demented patients participate meaningfully, such as in cooperating with a subjective screening instrument (e.g., the Geriatric Depression Scale)?

The usefulness of the Geriatric Depression Scale as a screening instrument has been widely debated. Two recent studies produced results suggesting that the Geriatric Depression Scale is not a useful

TABLE 2.1. Major Clinical Features Differentiating Pseudodementia from Dementia (Adapted from Wells, 1979)

<u>Pseudodementia</u>	<u>Dementia</u>
Rapid progression of symptoms	Slow progression of symptoms throughout course
History of previous psychiatric dysfunciton common	History of previous psychiatric dysfunction uncommon
Patients do complain of cognitive loss	Patients rarely complain of cognitive loss
Patients' efforts on tasks are variable	Patients conceal disability and struggle to perform tasks
Patients communicate a strong sense of distress	Patients often appear unconcerned
Loss of social skills often early and prominent	Social skills often retained
Attention and concentration often well preserved	Attention and concentration is usually faulty
"Don't know" answers typical	Near miss answers frequent
Memory loss for recent and remote events equally severe	Memory loss for recent events more severe than for remote events

instrument with a demented population (Burke et al., 1989; Kafonek et al., 1989). Burke et al. (1989) compared the depression scale scores in the mildly demented with psychiatric diagnoses. Kafonek et al. (1989) compared the scale's success in detecting depression with a standardized psychiatric interview among 70 patients newly admitted to a long-term-care facility. Sensitivity and specificity ratings determined by using a variety of cutoff scores were well below standard.

Other studies have provided evidence for reliability and validity in using the Geriatric Depression Scale with long-term-care demented elders. Lesher (1986), using a cutoff score of 11, found 100% sensitivity and 74% specificity in those with major depression. Split half-reliability was high (r = 0.84), as were alpha coefficient (r = 0.99) and test-retest reliability (r = 0.94). In the largest study of this kind, Parmelee, Katz, and Lawton (1989) found high internal consistency (reliability) and moderate-to-high correlations between staff ratings and Geriatric Depression Scale scores (concurrent validity). Our own study provided the only longitudinal data on the use of the Geriatric Depression Scale with demented elderly (Lichtenberg, Marcopulos, Steiner, and Tabscott, 1992). Using a cutoff score of 11, the sensitivity and specificity ratings were 82% and 85%, respectively.

SUMMARY

Neuropsychology, the use of expertise about brain-behavior relationships, was introduced as a valuable component of geriatric long-term-care treatment. The roles of a neuropsychologist were explored. In addition, an overview of how neuropsychology addresses primary referral questions was provided. As this chapter has shown, we have to identify the value of neuropsychology and to help broaden its usage in long-term care.

REFERENCES

Albert, M. Cognitive Functioning. In *Geriatric Neuropsychology*, edited by Albert, M. and Moss, M. (1988). New York: Guilford Press: 33-53.

Albert, M., and Moss, M. (Eds.) (1988). *Geriatric Neuropsychology*. New York: Guilford Press.

Blazer, D., Hughes, D., and George, L. (1987). The Epidemiology of Depression in an Elderly Community Population. *The Gerontologist, 27*, 281-287.

Burke, W., Houston, M., Boust, S., and Rosaforte, W. (1989). Use of the Geriatric Depression Scale in Dementia of the Alzheimer Type. *Journal of the American Geriatrics Society, 37*, 856-860.

Chenoweth, B., and Spencer, B. (1986). Dementia: The Experience of Family Caregivers. *The Gerontologist, 26*, 267-272.

The Diagnostic and Statistical Manual III-Revised. (1987). The American Psychiatric Association: Washington, DC.

Erber, J. (1974). Age Differences in Recognition Memory. *Journal of Gerontology, 29*, 177-181.

German, P.S., Shapiro, S., Skinner, E.A., Von Korff, M., Klein, L.E., Turner, R.W., Teitelbaum, M.L., Burke, J., and Burns, B.J. (1987). Detection and Management of Mental Health Problems of Older Patients by Primary Care Providers. *Journal of the American Medical Association, 257*, 489-493.

Gibson, A.J. (1981). A Further Analysis of Memory Loss in Dementia and Depression in the Elderly. *British Journal of Clinical Psychology, 20*, 179-185.

Greenwald, B.S., Kramer-Ginsberg, E., Marin, D.B., Laitman, L.B., Hermann, C.K., Mohs, R.C., and Davis, K.L. (1989). Dementia with Coexistent Major Depression. *American Journal of Psychiatry, 146*, 1472-1478.

Howell, S. (1972). Familiarity and Complexity in Perceptual Recognition. *Journal of Gerontology, 27*, 364-371.

Hunt, T., and Lindley, C. (Eds.) (1989). *Testing Older Adults.* PRO-ED: Texas.

Jenike, M. (1988). Depression and Other Psychiatric Disorders. In *Geriatric Neuropsychology,* edited by M. Albert and M. Moss. The Guilford Press: New York, 115-138.

Kafonek, S., Ettinger, W.H., Roca, R., Kittner, S., Taylor, N., and German, P.S. (1989). Instruments for Screening for Depression and Dementia in a Long-Term Care Facility. *Journal of the American Geriatrics Society, 37*, 29-34.

Kitchell, M.A., Barnes, R.F., Veith, R.C., Okimoto, J.T., and Raskind, M.A. (1982). Screening for Depression in Hospitalized Geriatric Medical Patients. *Journal of the American Geriatrics Society, 30*, 174-177.

Kramer, M., German, P., Anthony, J., Von Korff, M., and Skinner, E. (1985). Patterns of Mental Disorders Among the Elderly Residents of Eastern Baltimore. *Journal of the American Geriatrics Society, 33*, 236-245.

LaRue, A. (1989). Patterns of Performance on the Fuld Object Memory Evaluation in Elderly Inpatients with Depression or Dementia. *Journal of Clinical and Experimental Neuropsychology, 11*, 409-422.

LaRue, A., D'Elia, L., Clark, E., Spar, J., and Jarvik, L. (1986). Clinical Tests of Memory in Dementia, Depression and Healthy Aging. *Journal of Psychology and Aging, 1*, 69-77.

Lesher, E.L. (1986). Validation of the Geriatric Depression Scale Among Nursing Home Residents. *Clinical Gerontologist, 4*, 21-28.

Lezak, M. (1983). *Neuropsychological Assessment.* Oxford University Press: New York.

Lichtenberg, P., Heck, G., and Turner, A. (1988). Medical Psychotherapy with Elderly Psychiatric Inpatients: Uses of Paraprofessionals in Treatment. *Medical Psychotherapy, 1*, 87-93.

Lichtenberg, P., Marcopulos, B., McLain, C., Manning, C., and Sautter, S. (1992). A Comprehensive Neuropsychology Program in Geriatric Long-Term Care. *Medical Psychotherapy, 5*, 39-52.

Lichtenberg, P., Marcopulos, B., Steiner, D., and Tabscott, J. (1992). Comparison of the Hamilton Depression Rating Scale and the Geriatric Depression Scale: Detection of Depression in Dementia Patients. *Psychological Reports, 70*, 515-521.

Linn, L.S., and Yager, J. (1980). The Effect of Screening, Sensitization, and Feedback on Notation of Depression. *Journal of Medical Education, 55*, 942-949.

Marcopulos, B. (1989). Pseudodementia, Dementia and Depression: Test Differentiation. In *Testing Older Adults*, edited by T. Hunt and C. Lindley. PRO-ED: Texas, 70-91.

Martin, A., Brouwers, P., and LaLonde, F. (1986). Towards a Behavioral Typology of Alzheimer's Patients. *Journal of Clinical and Experimental Neuropsychology, 8*, 594-610.

McKhann, G., Drachman, D., Folstein, M., Katzman, R., Price, D., and Stadlan, E. (1984). Clinical Diagnosis of Alzheimer's Disease. *Neurology, 34*, 939-944.

McLean, S. (1987). Assessing Ddementia: Difficulties, Definitions, and Differential Diagnosis. *Australian and New Zealand Journal of Psychiatry, 21*, 142-174.

Moore, J.T., Silimperi, D.R., and Bobula, J.A. (1978). Recognition of Depression by Family Medicine Residents: The Impact of Screening. *Journal of Family Practice, 7*, 509-513.

Nielsen, A.C., and Williams, T.A. (1980). Depression in Ambulatory Medical Patients: Prevalence by Self-Report Questionnaire and Recognition by Nonpsychiatric Physicians. *Archives of General Psychiatry, 37*, 999-1004.

Norris, J.T., Gallagher, D., Wilson, A., and Winograd, C.H. (1987). Assessment of Depression in Geriatric Medical Outpatients: The Validity of Two Screening Measures. *Journal of the American Geriatrics Society, 35*, 989-995.

Okimoto, J.T., Barnes, R.F., Veith, R.C., Raskind, M.A., Inui, T.S., and Carter, W.B. (1982). Screening for Depression in Geriatric Medical Patients. *American Journal of Psychiatry, 139*, 799-802.

Parmelee, P.A., Katz, I.R., and Lawton, M.P. (1989). Depression Among Institutionalized Aged: Assessment and Prevalence Estimation. *Journal of Gerontology, 44*, M22-M29.

Rapp, S.R., and Davis, K.M. (1989). Geriatric Depression: Physicians' Knowledge, Perceptions, and Diagnostic Practices. *The Gerontologist, 29*, 252-257.

Rapp, S.R., Parisi, S.A., and Walsh, D.A. (1988). Psychological Dysfunction and Physical Health Among Elderly Medical Inpatients. *Journal of Consulting and Clinical Psychology, 56*, 851-855.

Rapp, S.R., Parisi, S.A., Walsh, D.A., and Wallace, C.E. (1988). Detecting Depression in Elderly Medical Inpatients. *Journal of Consulting and Clinical Psychology, 56*, 509-513.

Reifler, B., and Larson, E. (1989). Excess Disability in Dementia of the Alzheimer Type. In *Alzheimer's Disease Treatment and Family Stress: Directions for Research*, edited by E. Light and B. Lebowitz. U.S. Dept. of Health and Human Services: Rockville, MD.

Rovner, B.W., Broadhead, J., Spencer, M., Carson, K., and Folstein, M.F. (1989). Depression and Alzheimer's Disease. *American Journal of Psychiatry, 146*, 350-353.

Schuckit, M.A., Miller, P.L., and Hahlbohm, D. (1975). Unrecognized Psychiatric Illness in Elderly Medical-Surgical Patients. *Journal of Gerontology, 30*, 655-660.

Smyer, M. (1986). Providing Psychological Services in Nursing Homes. *The Clinical Psychologist*, 105-108.

Strub, R., and Black, F. (1985). *The Mental Status Examination in Neurology* (2nd edition). F.A. Davis Co: Philadelphia.

Waxman, H.M., and Carner, E.A. (1984). Physicians' Recognition, Diagnosis, and Treatment of Mental Disorders in Elderly Medical Patients. *The Gerontologist, 24*, 593-597.

Wedding, D., Horton, A., and Webster, J. (Eds.) (1986). *The Neuropsychology Handbook*. Springer Publishing: New York.

Weingartner, H., Cohen, R.M., Murphy, D.L., Martello, J., and Gerdt, C. (1981). Cognitive Processes in Depression. *Archives of General Psychiatry, 38*, 42-47.

Wells, C. (1979). Pseudodementia. *American Journal of Psychiatry, 136*, 895-900.

Williams, J.M., Little, M.M., Scates, S., and Blockman, N. (1987). Memory Complaints and Abilities Among Depressed Older Adults. *Journal of Consulting and Clinical Psychology, 55*, 595-598.

Chapter 3

Neuropsychological Test Batteries for Geriatric Long-Term Care

Neuropsychological testing in long-term care is most useful if the following three principles are utilized: (1) When there is any question of neurobehavioral deficits, a comprehensive assessment (Table 3.1) or an extended screening assessment should be utilized (Table 3.2); (2) A longitudinal approach, including followup screening exams (Table 3.3) and repeat comprehensive assessments, is the only reliable method of detecting cognitive changes; and (3) Assessment results must be tied to practical treatment planning. As can be seen in Table 3.1, the comprehensive assessment offers the most in-depth opportunity to sample all five areas of cognition (Benton and Hamsher, 1978; Brink et al., 1982; Fuld, 1977; Halstead and Wepman, 1959; Hooper 1958; Kaplan et al., 1978; Mattis, 1976; Nelson 1976; Reitan, 1958; Taylor, 1959; and Wechsler, 1981, 1987).

Comprehensive testing typically lasts 2-3 hours and requires the patient to be motivated and cooperative. Few patients refuse testing, and by using rest breaks, the assessments are typically completed during one or two sessions. Most of the tests described in Table 3.1 have normative data for the elderly. Several of the tests tap into memory and abstract reasoning. These skills are often the most vulnerable to brain impairment in the elderly, and thus are tested thoroughly. The information provided by testing assists with diagnosis, serves as a baseline against which later test results can be compared, and also displays the cognitive strengths to be used in intervention.

Some patients are already suffering from a diagnosed dementia. In the case where the diagnosis is well established and the patient

TABLE 3.1. Comprehensive Neuropsychological Battery to Assess Dementia
(Patients Allowed Two to Three Hours to Complete)

INSTRUMENTS

AREAS ASSESSED

General Intellectual/Cognitive Functioning

INSTRUMENTS	AREAS ASSESSED
Wechsler Adult Intelligence Scale-Revised (WAIS-R)	General measure of intelligence. Full scale verbal and performance IQ scores. Subtest scores (see below).
Dementia Rating Scale (DRS)	Basic meaure of cognitive functioning (e.g., attention, memory, visuomotor, abstract reasoning).

Attention

INSTRUMENTS	AREAS ASSESSED
Digit Span (WAIS-R)	Immediate auditory attention.
Visual Attention subtest (DRS)	Visual scanning.
Trails A	Simple visual motor tracking.

Language

INSTRUMENTS	AREAS ASSESSED
Aphasia Screening Test	Covers basic language areas: naming, reading, repetition, comprehension, expression.
Boston Naming Test	More difficult test of confrontational naming.
Vocabulary (WAIS-R)	Word Knowledge.

Memory

INSTRUMENTS	AREAS ASSESSED
Recall and recognition subtests (DRS)	Recall for sentences, recognition for designs and words.
Logical memory subtest (Wechsler Memory Scale-Revised)	Immediate and delayed recall for verbal contextual information.
Visual reproduction subtest (Wechsler Memory Scale-Revised)	Immediate and delayed recall for visuospatial material.

TABLE 3.1 (continued)

INSTRUMENTS	AREAS ASSESSED
Memory	
Fuld Object Memory Exam	Verbal learning and memory, recognition and delayed recall. Over five trials, learning 10 items that were handled and named.
Rey Auditory Verbal Learning Test	Learning 15 unrelated words over five trials. Short delay and recognition tasks as well.
Visuospatial	
Picture Completion (WAIS-R)	Recognizing missing details.
Picture Arrangement (WAIS-R)	Nonverbal test of social judgement and organization.
Digit Symbol (WAIS-R)	Visual-motor copying.
Hooper Visual Organization Test	Visuospatial integration task without a motor component.
Benton Visual Form Discrimination Test	Nonmotoric test of visuoperceptual skills.
Abstract Reasoning	
Similarities (WAIS-R)	Verbal abstract reasoning.
Block Design (WAIS-R)	Visuospatial abstract reasoning.
Trails B	Test of visuomotor tracking and mental flexibility.
Wisconsin Card Sorting Test	Test of mental flexibility and problem solving using feedback to modify performance.
(Nelson version)	
Controlled Oral Word Test	Test of verbal fluency and initiation.

TABLE 3.1 (continued)

INSTRUMENTS	**AREAS ASSESSED**
	Affect
Geriatric Depression Scale	Screening measure of depression
	Alcohol Abuse
CAGE Questionnaire	Screening test for alcohol abuse.

TABLE 3.2. Neuropsychological Screening Assessment for Dementia

INSTRUMENTS	**AREAS ASSESSED**
Dementia Rating Scale	Overall test of basic cognitive functioning. Taps into attention, memory, visuospatial, and abstract reasoning.
Locial Memory: Visual Reproduction (Wechsler Memory Scale-Revised)	Immediate and delayed verbal and visuospatial recall.
Fuld Object Memory Exam	Over five trials, learning 10 items that were handled and named.
Boston Naming Test	Test of confrontational naming.
Geriatric Depression Scale	Screening measure of depression.
CAGE	Screening measure for alcohol abuse.

cannot complete the comprehensive evaluation, the extended screening assessment is recommended (Table 3.2). This assessment takes about an hour to administer. Again, memory testing is heavily represented. These results can establish a baseline measure of cognition and guide treatment planning.

TABLE 3.3. Tests to Use in Six-Month Followups

Mini Mental State Exam

Mattis Organic Mental Syndrome Screening Exam

Dementia Rating Scale

Fuld Object Memory Exam

Geriatric Depression Scale

A brief followup screening exam is recommended every six months. In addition to the two tests described below, the Dementia Rating Scale and/or Fuld Memory Exam make excellent screening instruments. A screening instrument provides an objective way to determine a gross estimate of cognitive functioning. The necessary requirements for a screening instrument are brevity (15-25 minutes); reliability, with a significantly high hit rate; and test items that are relatively insensitive to disruption by anxiety or depression. There are numerous instruments available, but only two will be described here (see Lezak, 1983, for a complete review of tests).

Folstein's (1975) Mini Mental State Exam (MMSE) was designed to test cognitive functioning simply and rapidly, taking 5-10 minutes to administer. The maximum obtainable score is 30. MMSE generally differentiates between intact and demented elderly, using a cutoff score of 24 (Lezak, 1983). The majority of the items consist of orientation, language, and mental flexibility items. There is one item that taps recall memory and one item involving simple copying.

Mattis' (1976) Organic Mental Syndrome Screening Exam (MOMSSE) is a more extensive screening exam. One criticism of the MMSE has been that by being so easy, some early-stage dementia patients score in the intact range. The MOMSSE attempts to rectify this problem by estimating the patient's previous level of functioning and comparing this with test results. Educational level, occupation, age, and test score on the Information Subtest of the WAIS-R are all used to estimate previous functioning. Items on the MOMSSE are taken from several WAIS-R subtests, Benton's Geometric Figures and Eisenson's Test of Aphasia. Attention, abstract reasoning, recall memory, language tasks, and basic copying are all assessed. If on this followup testing a patient demonstrates significant improvement or decline, a more comprehensive evaluation should be considered.

Experience with providing followup neuropsychological assessments to long-term-care patients has underscored that caution is needed when interpreting results from a single assessment. These patients are frail, and they present dramatic medical, dietary, social, psychological, and psychiatric excess disabilities. These disabilities can have drastic effects on cognitive functioning. Longitudinal assessments, through a combination of full batteries and screening measures, are often necessary to detect change in cognitive functioning. This aspect of patient functioning is critical to treatment interventions, since cerebral dysfunction often leads to challenging behavior problems (Lezak, 1978). What follows are two case examples in which the referral question "Is the patient demented?" is addressed.

CASE 1:
A HIDDEN CASE OF EARLY PROGRESSIVE DEMENTIA

Mrs. M, a 78-year-old widow, slipped on the ice and broke her hip. The next day, she underwent surgery to set the hip. Her recovery was interrupted when she developed an episode of acute renal failure following the surgery; the hospital's nursing staff also noted that Mrs. M. seemed to be in a confused state of mind.

Mrs. M. lived alone prior to the surgery. Four of her five children lived out of town, and she was responsible for overseeing the affairs of the fifth adult child, a mentally retarded son. Because she was too weak physically to return home, she was sent to a long-term-care facility. Mrs. M. was socially adept and quickly became the favorite of many of the nursing staff. She had excellent verbal skills and loved to talk.

A routine screening neuropsychological evaluation, using the Dementia Rating Scale, was given. It was a surprise that some deficits were found. Thus, a comprehensive evaluation was completed. Mrs. M. was a high school graduate and had worked as a domestic most of her adult life. Her health was excellent, and she had no major chronic diseases. She seemed cheerful and carefree, but she quickly became anxious when she could not answer test questions. She had lived alone since the death of her husband in 1977, but she was unable to clearly relate how she spent her time. In addition, she revealed that people had been turning against her and she had no need for friends. Testing was completed; the results, deemed valid, are summarized in Table 3.4.

Interpretation of test results are best guided by the three questions introduced earlier. First, is there evidence of cerebral impairment? In reviewing Table 3.4, we can see that cognitive deficits are indeed in evidence. This leads to the question of what are the relative cognitive strengths and weaknesses. Cognitive strengths were found in tasks of attention and on most language tasks. Compared with normal elders, moderate-to-severe deficits were found in recall memory, naming, visuospatial tasks, and abstract reasoning. This widespread pattern of deficits was indicative of diffuse brain impairment (spread throughout the brain) rather than a discrete area of brain damage. When told of these results, Mrs. M. became upset with the examiner and accused him of wanting to ruin her life. She stated that she had no memory problems whatsoever.

How, then, can these test results lead to recommendations related to practical concerns. Indeed, the results of the evaluation had implications for the following:

- Competency to make own decisions
- Safety at home
- Financial management
- Ability to act as guardian for son

Mrs. M. performed poorly on many aspects of testing; however, due to her superior verbal skills and social graces, she appeared to be functioning normally. Test results indicated that she was suffering from a mild-to-moderate cognitive impairment. Was she as competent to handle her affairs at home as she appeared to be on the surface? Test results are equivocal on this matter, and they must be used as a guide in connection with other information. A second important piece of information was her own reaction. She denied having deficits and refused to use compensatory strategies. A third component was a more in-depth assessment of her community life. By interviewing others who knew Mrs. M., it was revealed that during the past year she had totally mismanaged her son's affairs

TABLE 3.4. Summary of Mrs. M's Neuropsychological Testing

General Intellectual Functioning:

Wechsler Adult Intelligence Scale Revised: Overall score in low average range, consistent with education and occupation.

Dementia Rating Scale: Overall score in mildly impaired range. Recall memory deficits noted.

Attention: (Digit Span, Letter Cancellation, Dementia Rating Scale, Trails A) Immediate auditory attention intact. Letter cancellation, visual attention intact. Simple visuomotor tracking was intact.

Language: (Boston Naming Test, Aphasia Screening Test) Severe naming problems, expression, comprehension intact, as was reading and writing.

Memory: (Wechsler Memory Scale-Revised, Fuld Object Memory Exam) Immediate recall for verbal contextual information was in the average range, but delayed recall was moderately impaired.

Recalling 10 items over 5 trials was significantly impaired, indicative of learning and recall memory deficits.

Visuospatial: (Hooper Visual Organization Test, Boston Naming Test) Integrating complex visual information was moderately impaired. Significant visuoperceptual errors were made in identifying objects from pictures.

Abstract Reasoning: (Similarities subtest of WAIS-R, Trials B, Nelson version of Wisconsin Card Sorting Test) Visuomotor tasks involving mental flexibility were severely impaired.

Verbal reasoning was concrete and moderately impaired.

Affect: No self-reported depression noted on the Geriatric Depression Scale. No vegetative symptoms of depression.

Substance Abuse: No indication of substance abuse on the CAGE Questionnaire.

and was being relieved of her guardianship duties. She had severed most of her friendships and had strained relations with her other children.

Mrs. M.'s memory problems made safety a concern. How would she remember to take the proper amount of medication at the proper time? She was at risk for mismanaging her checkbook, since her abstract reasoning skills were poor. I recommended that she have 24-hour supervision.

Mrs. M. later had a full battery of diagnostic tests and was diagnosed with Alzheimer's disease. Her illness progressed slowly, but her cognition declined steadily.

CASE 2: A CASE OF REVERSIBLE DEMENTIA

Mrs. E. was a high school graduate who had worked most of her adult life in a factory. After thirteen years of marriage, she divorced her husband–an alcohol abuser who physically abused her–and raised her three children by herself.

Mrs. E. was in her late sixties when she first entered a long-term-care facility. Two years before, she complained to her neighbor that an ex-coworker was out to harm her. She had had a brief psychiatric hospitalization and, upon her discharge, received a followup neurology and neuropsychology examination. She had severe cognitive dysfunction and was diagnosed with probable Alzheimer's disease. She refused medication for her many physical ailments. These included medicines for lung disease, asthma, and cardiac arrhythmia. She became so sick that she was placed on a respirator and was treated in ICU. One month later, she entered our long-term-care facility. A month after that, she underwent a comprehensive neuropsychological assessment. She was fully cooperative with the assessment.

In Table 3.5, the results of Mrs. E.'s longitudinal comprehensive evaluations can be found (including those she had prior to entering long-term care). Especially striking were improvements in memory and verbal learning, visuospatial skills, and in general functioning– which was inconsistent with a diagnosis of progressive dementia. Problem-solving skills requiring visuomotor tracking and mental flexibility remained deficient.

There were several conclusions and practical recommendations directly made from this assessment. Her areas of cognitive strength indicated that Mrs. E. should be functioning independently for most self-care tasks. A daily program to assess independent functioning was thus initiated. She began caring for her own ADLs, doing her

TABLE 3.5. Mrs. E.'s Longitudinal Results on Neuropsychological Tests

Area of Cognitive Functioning	Testing #1 Results from 1988	Testing #2 Results from 1989
Attention:	Intact simple auditory and visuomotor attention.	Intact simple auditory and visuomotor attention.
Language:	Severe dysnomia. All else intact.	Mild dysnomia. All else intact.
Memory:	Immediate recall severely impaired. Verbal learning severly impaired.	Intact immediate and delayed recall. Above average verbal learning.
Visuospatial:	Severly impaired simple copying skills. Severely impaired visual-organizational skills.	Intact simple copying. Mildly impaired visual-organizational skills.
Abstract Reasoning:	Severly impaired verbal fluency, visuomotor tracking and mental flexibility.	Intact verbal fluency. Severly impaired visuomotor tracking and mental flexibility.
General Intellectual Functioning:	Borderline intellectual functioning.	Low average intellectual functioning.
Affect:	Not evaluated.	No depression

laundry, creating her own activities schedule, and requesting medications at the appropriate time and in the correct quantities. Neuropsychological deficits in visuomotor tracking and mental flexibility indicated that a return to driving a car was not recommended. After a three-week successful trial of this program–and with her vastly improved health–Mrs. E. returned home.

A small but significant percentage of long-term-care patients return to an independent living situation. As part of a comprehensive approach to neuropsychology in long-term care, home assessments are necessary. In Table 3.6, a home assessment outline is presented. This is based on work by Kapust and Weintraub (1988). The assessment utilizes interview techniques and specific tasks to determine the early success or failure of a return to the community, and to offer suggestions for improved living.

Two weeks after her discharge, Mrs. E. was visited for a home assessment. She was neat and clean, as was her apartment. She accurately told us her daily appointments and was using lists to help her complete chores. A logical system for taking medications was demonstrated. Mrs. E. was unable to complete a driver's evaluation and was resigned to using the bus system for most of her transportation. Adequate strategies for emergencies were also demonstrated.

TABLE 3.6. Home Assessment Outline

I. Inspect environment, appearance of those living there.

II. Tell me about your typical day?

    1. Patient describes bathing and dressing
    2. Patient describes eating (meals and snacks)
    3 Patient describes social activity
    4. Interviewer checks for depression: Energy, Sleep, Crying, Appetite

III. Complete 5 tasks

    1. Prepare a cup of tea
    2. Locate phone book, look up number for time and temperature and dial it
    3. Find keys, hammer, general items
    4. Direct examiner on tour of house
       a. Look in medicine cabinet
       b. Look in refrigerator, freezer, pantry
    5. Ask about strategies for emergency
       a. Who to call/ ask for help
       b. Funds

Table 3.6 (continued)

IV. Compensatory Strategies

1. How to keep track of appointments
2. How to remember to take medicines
3. How to keep account of spending money
4. Usage of cane, walker, wheelchair, special bed etc.

Clearly, the return to independent living was warranted. When Mrs. E. died due to pulmonary disease, an autopsy revealed that she did not have Alzheimer's disease. Her dementia, caused by her lung disease, reversed when she became physically well.

ASSESSING DEPRESSION

As was brought out in the previous chapter, detecting depression in long-term-care patients is vitally important. Because of its demonstrated usefulness, the Geriatric Depression Scale is presented in detail.

Classic depressive symptomatology appears in three domains: affective (sadness, tearfulness); cognitive (worthlessness, hopelessness); and somatic (fatigue, insomnia). The authors of the Geriatric Depression Scale (Brink et al., 1982; Yesavage et al., 1983) had as their goal the creation of a depression scale that was developed using an elderly population, as opposed to such commonly used instruments as the Beck and Zung scales, which were developed on younger subjects. Three steps were taken in creating the Geriatric Depression Scale (GDS). First, 100 statements were generated that depressives were likely to endorse. They gave these to 46 subjects and then narrowed them down to the 30 items that best correlated with the total score. The median correlation was 0.67 (range = 0.47-0.83). None of the items measuring somatic symptomatology remained; that is, the somatic items did not help with diagnostic specificity. In the second stage of development, the authors gave the 30-item scale to 20 non-depressed and 20 depressed elders. Each subject was also given the Zung Self-Rating Scale and obtained an observer rating on the Hamilton Depression Inventory. The Geriatric Depression Scale was the best in terms of distinguishing between groups. Third, the number of subjects was increased to 40 normals and 60 depressives. The severity of depression was determined and, again, the Geriatric Depression Scale was the best in classifying severity of depression. Using a cutoff score of ten produced an 84% sensitivity rate and a 95% specificity rate, while a cutoff score of 14 produced an 80% sensitivity rate and a 100% specificity rate. Followup studies by Hyer and Blount (1984) and Norris et al. (1987) produced further evidence of the validity of the Geriatric Depression Scale with older long-term-care patients and with medical outpatients.

The Geriatric Depression Scale offers an instrument that, due to its yes-or-no format, is easy to give and score. Apart from being used to detect depression in long-term-care patients, the instrument's penetrating questions can serve as a springboard to further discussion.

The following case represents common findings in depressed, medically ill long-term-care patients.

CASE 3:
DEPRESSION AND THE PHYSICALLY ILL ELDER

Mrs. S. entered a long-term-care facility after suffering a severe leg fracture when she ran her automobile into a car parked on the side of the road. She was a divorced 83-year-old retired executive secretary who had been living alone. She had two children; her eldest daughter helped her with financial planning and some errands. Mrs. S.'s medical problems included congestive heart failure, ileus, hypertension, and a lifelong history of rheumatoid arthritis. Due to weakness and loss of function in her leg, Mrs. S. was unable to drive, so she opted to enter a long-term-care facility. The nursing staff noticed memory lapses and periods of confusion in Mrs. S. and wondered if she was suffering from dementia.

Mrs. S. was uncomfortable about neuropsychological testing, but she agreed to complete an extended screening evaluation (see Table 3.2). Mrs. S. was a graduate from both high school and business college. She quit her job in her late twenties, when she had children. For 25 years, she was happily married to a successful engineer. He began to abuse alcohol and soon lost his job and left the family. At that time, she returned to work. Mrs. S. was exceedingly formal, but cooperative. When frustrated by a test question, she would state that "this is the last thing I would be interested in."

The most striking results of her neuropsychological assessment was her score on the Geriatric Depression Scale of severe depression. Although she did not suffer severe sleep or appetite problems, she was unhappy, downhearted, feeling blue, hopeless, and helpless. She often wanted to cry, but could not. Mrs. S. also noticed reduced concentration abilities and lowered energy. Cognitively, Mrs. S. displayed mild recall-memory impairments and mild naming problems. Compared with the first case presented in this chapter, the deficits displayed by Mrs. S. were not as great as those of Mrs. M.

Upon providing feedback of Mrs. S.'s depression to her physician and the staff, they were in disbelief. "But she never cried or complained," they argued. Table 3.7 lists the common characteristics of depressed elderly whose depression is not obvious at all. These patients, as Mrs. S. demonstrated, display no tears and voice no complaints. Their affect visibly brightens upon interview, since they are often emotionally guarded.

A followup meeting with Mrs. S. was conducted, and feedback provided, regarding the results of the evaluation. She readily concurred that she was depressed and stated that she had been for a long time. She was in crisis: her identity was threatened by the loss of independence and it overwhelmed her. She completed three months of psychotherapy, at which time her depression and memory disturbance subsided.

CASE 4: DEPRESSION AND DEMENTIA

Mr. C. is a 75-year-old single white male who was admitted to an acute hospital unit due to an inability to care for himself. Mr. C.'s main occupation was working on the family farm. Eight years prior to his hospitalization, his family noticed that he was forgetful and confused at times. He began talking to himself, refused to bathe, and became less able to care for himself. The brother with whom the patient lived went away for two weeks; upon his return, he found Mr. C. totally disheveled, malnourished, agitated, and wandering. Mr. C. was then brought to a long-term-care facility. Upon entering the facility Mr. C. weighed 124 pounds, was anemic, and seemed to be suffering from an agitated depression. His CT scan showed cerebral atrophy.

Six weeks later, he completed his first neuropsychological assessment (see Table 3.8 for longitudinal results). On the Dementia Rating Scale and MMSE, his scores were consistent with severe global cerebral dysfunction. On the MOMSSE, he scored in the below-average range for general knowledge and in the defective range for verbal abstract reasoning and immediate auditory attention. Mr. C. scored in the severely depressed range on the Geriatric Depression Scale. Mr. C. had many severe behavioral problems. He was constantly wandering and intrusive to the point where he was physically attacked by another patient. He was also extremely restless and constantly moved furniture. Nortriptyline was used to treat his depression, and a low dose of Thioridazine was used to calm him.

Mr. C. demonstrated considerable improvement within six months, particularly in the area of his social and affective functioning. His wandering decreased, and his intrusiveness subsided. He was no longer depressed (GDS = 9), was eating well, was neat and clean, and weighed 144 pounds. Cognitive improvement was also noted with significant gains on his Dementia Rating Scale and MMSE scores.

Mr. C.'s cognitive abilities were particularly sensitive to physical illness, which resulted in excess disability. One month, he demonstrated a decline on cognitive screening tests. He scored a 10 on the MMSE. At this time, it was found that he was suffering from dehydration as a result of his diuretic. His Lasix dosage was reduced, and his functioning improved again.

Throughout his final five months in the long-term-care facility, Mr. C. continued to show astonishing improvement. Another thorough neuropsychological assessment was performed. His Dementia Rating Scale score had increased again and was in the mild-to-moderately impaired range. On tests of word knowledge, attention, and visuospatial abstract reasoning, he scored in the below-average range. As measured by the Fuld Object Memory Exam, his memory was also mildly impaired.

TABLE 3.7. Common Characteristics of Hidden Depression in Physically Ill Elderly

Behavioral Patterns:

Lack of tearfulness
Voice no complaints
Brighten upon interview
Emotionally guarded
Inconsistent performance on tasks

Psychological Symptoms:

History of early and recent losses
Cognitive errors (Beck's triad of symptoms)
Significant reduced pleasant events (Lewinsohn's model of
     depression)

Neuropsychological Deficits:

Memory impairment
Abstract reasoning deficits

TABLE 3.8. Mr. C.'s Longitudinal Results on Selected Neuropsychological Tests

Date of Testing	Test Name	Test Score
9/88	Dementia Rating Scale	64
	Mini Mental State	12
	Geriatric Depression Scale	21
3/89	Dementia Rating Scale	107
	Mini Mental State	27
	Geriatric Depression Scale	9
9/89	Dementia Rating Scale	118
	Mini Mental State	30
	Geriatric Depression Scale	3

Mr. C.'s case is an example of excess disability secondary to depression in a demented individual. Upon entering long-term-care, his behavior was typical of patients with advanced Alzheimer's. His cognitive abilities were severely impaired, and he displayed a myriad of behavioral problems (wandering, intrusiveness, etc.). As his depression and malnutrition were treated, he became able to develop trusting relationships with the nursing staff and to improve his eating and grooming. His cognitive abilities steadily improved.

SUMMARY

This chapter focused on specific neuropsychological tests that are especially useful with geriatric patients. Tests that provide for comprehensive or screening evaluations were chosen because of their value with long-term-care patients. Case examples illustrated the complex and often confusing neuropsychological problems experienced by geriatric patients.

REFERENCES

Benton, A., and Hamsher, K. (1978). *Multilingual Aphasia Examination.* University of Iowa Press: Iowa City.

Brink, T., Yesavage, J., Lum, G., Heersema, P., Addey, M., and Rose, T. (1982) Screening Tests for Geriatric Depression. *Clinical Gerontologist, 1,* 37-41.

Folstein, M., Folstein, S., and McHugh, P. (1975). Mini Mental State: A Practical Method for Grading the Cognitive State of Patients for the Clinician. *Journal of Psychiatric Research, 12,* 189.

Fuld, P. (1977). *Fuld Object Memory Evaluation.* Saul R. Korey Dept. of Neurology: New York.

Halstead, W., and Wepman, J. (1959). The Halstead-Wepman Aphasia Screening Test. *Journal of Speech and Hearing Disorders, 14,* 9-15.

Hooper, H. (1958). *The Hooper Visual Organization Test.* Western Psychological Services: Los Angeles.

Hyer, L., and Blount, J. (1984). Concurrent and Discriminant Validities of the Geriatric Depression Scale with Older Psychiatric Inpatients. *Psychological Reports, 54,* 611-616.

Kaplan, E., Goodglass, H., and Weintraub, S. (1978). *The Boston Naming Test.* E. Kaplan and H. Goodglass: Boston.

Kapust, L., and Weintraub, S. (1988). The Home Visit: Field Assessment of Mental Status Impairment in the Elderly. *The Gerontologist, 28,* 112-115.

Lezak, M. (1978). Living with the Characterologically Altered Brain Injured Patient. *Journal of Clinical Psychiatry, 39,* 592-598.

Lezak, M. (1983). *Neuropsychological Assessment.* Oxford University Press: New York.

Mattis, S. (1976). Mental Status Examination for Organic Mental Syndrome in the Elderly Patient. In Bellak, A. and Karagan, B. (Eds.) *Geriatric Psychiatry,* Grune and Stratton: New York, 77-101.

Nelson, H. (1976) A Modified Card Sorting Test Sensitive to Frontal Lobe Defects. *Cortex, 12,* 313-324.

Norris, J., Gallagher, D., Wilson, A., and Winograd, C. (1987). Assessment of Depression in Geriatric Medical Outpatients: The Validity of Two Screening Measures. *Journal of the American Geriatrics Society, 35,* 989-995.

Reitan, R. (1958). Validity of the Trail Making Test as an Indicator of Brain Damage. *Perceptual and Motor Skills, 8,* 271-276.

Taylor, E. (1959). *The Appraisal of Children with Cerebral Deficits.* Harvard University Press: Cambridge, Mass.

Wechsler, D. (1981). *WAIS-R Manual.* Psychological Corporation: New York.

Wechsler, D. (1987). *The Wechsler Memory Scale-Revised.* Psychological Corporation: New York.

Yesavage, J., Brink, T., Rose, T., Lum, O., Huang, V., Adez, M., and Leirer, V. (1983). Development and Validation of a Geriatric Depression Screening Scale: A Preliminary Report. *Journal of Psychiatric Research, 17,* 37-49.

Chapter 4

Creating an Effective
Interdisciplinary Team

Innovations to improve the quality of geriatric long-term care can occur only by involving the nursing assistants and licensed practical nurses. In this chapter, studies that have investigated the link between quality of care and the roles of nursing assistant and licensed practical nurse will be reviewed. In addition, past uses of training and organizational restructuring in attempts to improve care will be discussed. The interdisciplinary team will be examined as an opportunity to promote quality through training and organizational restructuring. Three years of a deliberate implementation of interdisciplinary team functioning will then be described in detail.

THE ROLE OF NURSING ASSISTANTS AND LICENSED PRACTICAL NURSES IN QUALITY CARE

Licensed practical nurses and nursing assistants hold the vast majority (88%) of full-time positions and over half of all positions in geriatric long-term care (Kasteler et al., 1979; Smyer, Cohn, and Brannon, 1988). Nursing assistants outnumber licensed practical nurses four to one, and licensed practical nurses outnumber registered nurses by a margin of one and a half to one. Two studies employing momentary time-sampling methodology provided insight as to how nursing assistants and licensed practical nurses spend their time (Burgio et al., 1990; Kahana and Kiyak, 1984). Patient care and interacting with patients were the predominant activities, and, for the most part, the staff were rated as treating their patients as equals.

It is thus remarkable to realize that although they provide most of the patient care, nursing assistants are discouraged from verbalizing their ideas about patient care and are not even considered as part of the treating health-care team (Faulkner, 1985; Kasteler et al., 1979; Sbordone and Sterman, 1983; Schwartz, 1984; Smith, Discenza, and Saxberg, 1978; and Stein, Linn, and Stein, 1986). So while nursing assistants are heavily involved in difficult patient care, they often feel isolated and neglected.

Turnover among the nursing assistants is incredibly high, is costly to the institution, and has considerable effect on quality care (Kasteler et al., 1979; Schwartz, 1974; Smyer, Cohn, and Brannon, 1988; Waxman, Carner, and Berkenstock, 1984). Kasteler et al. (1979) and Schwartz (1974) reported turnover of the nursing assistants at 75%, whereas Waxman, Carner, and Berkenstock found it to vary from 5% to 76% among seven long-term-care facilities. Kasteler et al. interviewed 426 terminated nursing assistants to identify the problems they encountered. A majority of the nursing assistants were disenchanted with the understaffing and overwork, along with such organizational problems as poor supervision and communication. Waxman, Carner, and Berkenstock concluded that a rigid organizational structure, one that did not allow the nursing assistants to communicate with professional staff, was a major contributor to turnover. Smith, Discenza, and Saxberg (1978) found that 71% of the nursing assistants and licensed practical nurses had contact with the Director of Nursing only through their charge nurses.

Turnover is costly not only financially but also in the delivery of quality services. Barton (1977) stressed the need to plan for communication among different subgroups in long-term care or else prepare to suffer from spiraling conflict. Stein, Linn, and Stein (1986) studied ten homes and 239 patients to discover the relationship between patient perceptions of staff and the quality of care. Their findings echoed Barton's conclusions: higher-quality long-term-care homes allowed nursing assistants to become significantly involved in decision making. Staff satisfaction was also directly related to quality of care. Kahana and Kiyak (1984) found that those staff who were most satisfied showed the most positive psychosocial interactions with patients. In his recommendations to reduce turnover, Schwartz (1974) identified the need for ongoing training.

He saw gaps in the knowledge necessary for quality service delivery.

GAPS IN KNOWLEDGE
AMONG NURSING ASSISTANTS

Behavioral disorders, agitation, disorientation, and depression are the most difficult patient problems for long-term-care staff (Lebray, 1979; Smyer, Cohn, and Brannon, 1988). Long-term-care staff are not well equipped with knowledge regarding treatment of these problems (Caston, 1983; Cohn et al., 1987). Whereas long-term-care administrators believed that they were providing staff training in many of these areas, less than 40% of the nursing assistants stated that they had received training in disorientation, depression, and delusions. Less than 20% reported receiving training in grief, drug misuse, family concerns, and sexuality (Cohn et al., 1987). Caston (1983) reported that even directors of nursing and charge nurses were poor at recognizing symptoms of mental illness in long-term-care patients.

Table 4.1 lists the most common difficulties nursing assistants and practical nurses face. Turnover, job dissatisfaction, being excluded from organizational and treatment decisions, and having a lack of knowledge about their patients' problems are areas that need to be addressed. The next two sections will describe training programs and organizational changes that have attempted to rectify these concerns.

Filling the Psychosocial Gap: Training

There has been a growing emphasis on preservice and inservice training to nursing assistants that started in the early 1970s and was heightened by the passage of the Omnibus Budget Reconciliation Act of 1987 that made 75 hours of inservice on physical and psychosocial issues mandatory. In this discussion, studies documenting training needs will be reviewed first, and then model training programs will be presented.

TABLE 4.1. Common Problems in Long-Term-Care Staff: Nursing Assistants and Licensed Practical Nurses

High Turnover

Job dissatisfaction

Exclusion from organizational decisions

Lack of communication between levels of staff

Gaps in knowledge of behavioral problems

Inadequate staffing patterns

Past studies documented that not only were staff poorly informed about behavioral problems but actually acted in a manner that encouraged passivity and dependency in their patients (Baltes, 1983; Cohn et al., 1987; Guy and Morice, 1985; Meunier and Holmes, 1987; and Spore, Smyer, and Cohn, 1991). In a series of careful studies, Baltes and her colleagues looked at sequential observations of interactions between the long-term-care patients and their social partners. They found that the long-term-care environment supported dependent self-care behaviors. It was common, for example, to see a long-term-care patient who was not eating at meal time to be approached by staff and fed, while another patient attempting to eat received no praise for their efforts and in fact was ignored.

Nursing assistants in long-term care do not often have a good working knowledge of communication and behavior management principles. In a study of 35 long-term-care facilities, only 54% used behavior management plans. The nursing assistants were estimated to carry out 63% of the behavior management programs, despite the fact that only 16% of the staff had received training in behavior management (Guy and Morice, 1985).

Specific methods for assessing nursing assistants' knowledge of problems have recently been developed. Meunier and Holmes (1987) created the Behavioral Knowledge Questionnaire (BKQ), a 31-item multiple-choice test designed to measure skills for working with behaviorally disruptive elderly. Compared with psychologists, the 62 nursing assistants and 71 social service/activity directors scored poorly on the exam. One drawback of the BKQ, however, was that the authors did not provide psychometric data on the instrument. Spore, Smyer, and Cohn (1991) recently improved the BKQ, and they also developed the Mental Health Caregiving Questionnaire (MHQ). The MHQ covers general behavioral management for problems of depression, disorientation, and agitation. This 20-item multiple-choice test displayed moderate internal consistency (alpha = 0.50) and test/retest reliability (r = 0.63). Evidence for construct validity was displayed when psychological consultants scored significantly better than did nursing assistants. Content validity was derived by pre-posttesting nursing assistants prior to and after a training module. Nursing assistants who underwent the training showed significantly improved scores.

Model Training Efforts

Early, small-scale efforts in the 1980s explored whether training led to cognitive gains in the nursing assistants (Almquist and Bates, 1980; Nigl and Jackson, 1981). The Dade County, Florida, special-project grant provided staff training for six nursing assistants and licensed practical nurses during six one-hour didactic sessions. The first half of the instruction focused on an introduction to aging and the physiology of aging, and the second half focused on physical and psychosocial problems of the elderly (Almquist and Bates, 1980). Pre- and posttesting indicated cognitive gains by the trainees, although no statistical analysis was applied.

Nigl and Jackson (1981) utilized both a four-week training course on behavior management and an A-B-A design to assess the course's impact on patient care. Their training of nursing assistants included three components: (1) a seminar on learning and behavior; (2) practice monitoring and recording behaviors; and (3) practice delivering reinforcers. Following the training, the effects of staff reinforcement of patient behaviors was measured. Six long-term-care patients, all with a lengthy history of psychosis and psychiatric treatment, received ten days of positive reinforcement from the nursing assistants for appropriate social behaviors (e.g., speaking, communicating). This was followed by ten days without the reinforcement and a second ten-day period with positive reinforcement. Target behaviors were significantly higher in the reinforcement condition than in the no-reinforcement condition, indicating that the training was effective.

Patterson and Gurian (1976) described their experience as one of the National Institutes of Mental Health's (NIMH's) six long-term-care education projects across the United States. Sixty-eight social workers and nurses completed a ten-week "how to teach" course in order to increase education efforts by long-term-care facilities aimed at mental-health problems. Their survey results, taken a year after the training, were disappointing: only 20% taking the course used the ideas in their own long-term-care facility. The authors hypothesized that lack of organizational support in the long-term-care facilities and the brief length of the course were key factors in the discouraging findings.

Larger and more intensive training efforts have demonstrated a number of different ways to institute effective training (Burgio, Whitman, and Reid, 1983; Burgio and Burgio, 1990; Chartock et al., 1988; Cohn et al., 1987; Mallya and Fitz, 1987; Smyer, Brannon, and Cohn, 1992). These are highlighted in Table 4.2.

Burgio and his colleagues have spent a decade carefully studying the participative management approach. Burgio, Whitman, and Reid (1983) introduced their approach in a study to increase direct-care staff's interaction with mentally retarded residents. The key concepts of the participative management approach in this case were to help the staff set their own goals for the number of interactions; self-monitoring by staff of their own performance; the staff's graphing of their own data; and self-praise when the goal was met. Trained observers (90% reliability) used momentary time sampling to measure the quantity of the staff's interactions with patients prior to and during the participative management approach. The results were encouraging. At baseline, staff had a 19% interaction rate, compared with a 40% interaction rate during participative management. Burgio and Burgio (1990) utilized training, self-monitoring, and social rewards in a long-term-care facility to improve nursing assistant compliance with a toileting program that significantly improved patient dryness. Burgio and Burgio (1990) recommended three components of training in long-term-care: (1) antecedent instruction (training); (2) monitoring of staff performance; and (3) application of consequences (rewards for staff meeting goals).

TABLE 4.2. A Variety of Effective Training Methods

Author	Method
1. Burgio	Participant management approach; nursing assistants self selection of goals; self monitoring and developing reward systems to improve staff behavior.
2. Chartock et al.	56 hours of training (seminar and small group exercises) to increase knowledge, to broaden staff role in mental health treatment, enhance teamwork and improve staff communication skills.
3. Nigl and Jackson	Training on behavior management to include: seminars; guided practice of monitoring and recording; guided practice delivering rewards.
4. Mallya and Fitz	Special assignments of paraprofessionals to help with 10 clients' mental health problems; Early intensive training and ongoing, long term supervision.
5. Smyer, Cohn, Brannon Cohn, Horgas and Mariske	Five 1 1/2 hour seminars on depression, disorientation, agitation; homework and class participation exercises.

Chartock et al. (1988) described their five-year project that culminated at four New York State long-term-care facilities. The emphasis was on training, teamwork, and organizational problems. Fifty-six hours of didactics–including five modules of training (normal aging, communications, mental impairment, team building, and working with families)–were used with 350 professional and paraprofessional staff to address four main goals (see Table 4.2). Their research methodology included pre- and posttesting as well as supervisor ratings of nursing assistants' performance two months after the training ended. The results of testing indicated that nursing assistants made significant gains in identifying depression and dementia. In addition, supervisors reported that 93% of the nursing assistants showed improved communication skills with their patients.

Mallya and Fitz (1987) introduced the St. Louis Regional Community Placement Program, whose focus was on the therapeutic needs of the mentally ill elderly. The authors provided training to a select group of paraprofessional staff and then helped to develop, implement, and evaluate treatment plans. Monthly training was provided on topics such as normal aging, mental illness, communication skills, behavior management, rehabilitation process, and family relationships. The project staff identified 44 areas of patient behavior that could be improved. The program was evaluated by comparing ratings of patient improvement in long-term-care facilities using the program (n = 3) with those that were not (n = 1). Nine behavioral areas were significantly improved in the experimental group (versus the control group). Blind ratings, however, were not used, since the project staff made the ratings themselves. This methodological weakness calls into question the findings because experimenter bias could account for the group differences.

The most extensive training program is the Penn State Nursing Home Project. Interdisciplinary professionals from Penn State produced a number of papers describing the need for training, developing questionnaires to assess mental-health knowledge, and evaluating the training (Brannon et al., 1988; Cohn et al., 1987; Cohn, Horgas, and Marsiske, 1990; Smyer, Cohn, and Brannon, 1988; Smyer, Brannon, and Cohn, 1992; and Spore, Smyer, and Cohn, 1991). Their program intervention was two-pronged: (1) to provide training and (2) to address organizational problems.

Cohn, Horgas, and Marsiske (1990) utilized five 1 1/2-hour training sessions (monthly) in an attempt to improve nursing assistants' knowledge at four long-term-care facilities. Training focused on problems with depression, disorientation, agitation, and behavior management techniques. On the first and fifth session, the nursing assistants completed a questionnaire on knowledge of normal aging. Specific behavior management techniques were evaluated by presenting a case vignette to the assistants. The nursing assistants' overall knowledge significantly improved, and a positive correlation was found between test scores and the assistants' self-assessed performance.

Smyer, Brannon, and Cohn (1992) described further program evaluation research. In their sample, nursing assistants from three long-term-care facilities received intervention, while one facility served as a control group. Measurements at the participating facilities were taken prior to the interventions, immediately following the intervention, and three and six months following the interventions. The training was as described above. Outcome measures included the MHQ and supervisors' ratings of nursing assistants' performance (Caregiver Rating Scale), which was used to assess actual behavior change. Inter-rater reliability on the Caregiver Rating Scale was low (0.30 to 0.53). The results indicated significant improvement on the MHQ at the training sites, compared with the control sample. There was, however, no change in nursing assistant performance when rated by the supervisors. This latter finding may be due to the unreliability of the rating scale. That is, rater bias may mask real changes in the nursing assistants.

Summary and Critique

In the last decade, several innovative and outstanding training programs have been developed. The programs reviewed have demonstrated that with good training, nursing assistants can significantly increase their knowledge of their patients' psychosocial problems. The best model of training is didactic instruction coupled with supervised hands-on practice. As Smyer, Brannon, and Cohn (1992) found, however, training does not automatically lead to improved performance. It is not enough to provide good training.

There must be three additional components to any training interventions. First, organizational issues must be addressed. Two of the training programs recognized and incorporated this aspect (Chartock et al., 1988; Smyer, Brannon, and Cohn, 1992). Without this component, the problems leading to staff turnover (i.e., time management, communication patterns in facilities, and conflicts between staff) overwhelm any training effort and make the knowledge to nursing assistants seem remote and unimportant. Second, contact must be ongoing. A brief, one-shot training program that does not have followup training to help implement knowledge is doomed to have minimal impact. Long-term-care patients present difficult problems. The nature of the interventions, although often simple, are not simple-minded. The long-term-care staff needs guidance in creating practical interventions. In addition, interventions do not always work immediately, and thus problem-solving skills and flexibility are needed. Even when interventions work well, it should not be assumed that they will retain their efficacy forever. Treatment programs must change when their usefulness wears away. Good communication among staff is vital as well, because most problems are multifaceted and multidisciplinary. Clearly, ten hours of training, or even fifty, does not address these problems. Third, more than "token" administrative support for improving psychosocial functioning is needed from long-term-care administrators. This has become obvious to all who provide consultation to long-term-care facilities. Obtaining this support often entails developing a strong relationship over many months with administrators of facilities and their departments. If the contact is brief, such as in a one-shot training program, it is difficult to get administrators to implement what is being taught. In sum, training for nursing assistant staff is a necessary, but not sufficient, condition for improving psychosocial care. Attention is now turned to the efforts of consultants to long-term care who intervened by addressing organizational issues.

ORGANIZATIONAL INTERVENTIONS IN LONG-TERM CARE

The best way to highlight the importance of organizational influence on staff is to review consulting efforts that failed to address these concerns. Ferrington and Panicucci (1986) reported on the difficulties that arise when time spent on long-term-care facility projects is valued differently by different groups. As mentioned previously, Patterson and Gurian's (1976) training was essentially ignored due to organizational roadblocks. Since, as Barton (1977) pointed out, supervisors often dominate the communication networks in long-term care, employee feedback is generally excluded.

In discussing the management of nursing assistants in long-term care, Reagan (1986) cited organizational factors, setting clear goals, and allowing for interaction within the health-care team as the most important factors in improving performance and reducing turnover. In the same study, the authors noted that the nursing assistants rated increased and improved supervision as their most pressing need.

Innovative programs that are effective are often so because organizational changes occur concurrently (Chartock et al., 1988). Chartock and her colleagues' most successful training programs created organizational change. Some of these changes included: increasing bath time, so that nursing assistants could attend to the patients' emotional needs as well as their physical ones; making mental-health issues a more frequent focus in patient conferences; and including nursing assistants in treatment-team meetings.

Three innovative and well-conceived organizational approaches are reviewed in Table 4.3.

Sbordone and Sterman (1983) cited their colleagues' failure to recognize organizational issues as the chief reason for the failure to have behavioral management programs implemented during the 1970s. Furthermore, they argued that, with high turnover rates running rampant, staff training effects would certainly be minimal. Their 12-week consultative intervention was aimed at improving communication, especially among members in different hierarchical levels in a 188-bed long-term-care facility. First, they interviewed administrators and then each employee to identify goals and objectives, staff problems, work responsibilities, supervisory relationships, and communication patterns. In the context of wanting to improve staff morale and reduce turnover, seven weekly meetings (including all shifts) were held. The head long-term-care administrator and Director of Nursing attended the last two meetings, resulting in a program of positive reinforcement for excellent work. Sbordone and Sterman emphasized the distorted paternalism of the administration regarding nursing assistants and the rare inclusion of nursing assistant input into patient care, despite their doing most of the work. The authors measured turnover rates to assess their effectiveness. Whereas there was a turnover rate of 70% the year prior to the consultation, it was only 33% in the three quarters following the

TABLE 4.3. Organizational Approaches Used by Mental-Health Consultants in Long-Term Care

Author	Method
Sbordone and Sterman (1983)	Focus on communication with specific emphasis on improving communication among different hierarchies.
Holtz (1982)	Herzberg's Motivation-Hygiene Theory: Motivation: achievement recognition, work itself, responsibility, advancement. Hygiene: company policy, supervision, salary, interpersonal relationships, working conditions.
Brannon et al. (1988)	Hackman's and Oldham's (1975)
Brannon and Bodnar (1988)	Job Redesign: skill variety, task
Smyer, Brannon and Cohn (1990)	identity, task significance,
Rountree and Deckard (1986)	autonomy, feedback.

consultation. Other researchers have focused on different aspects of organizational makeup in long-term care.

Holtz (1982) used Herzberg's motivation-hygiene theory to assess organizational issues in long-term care. The theory states that if five hygiene factors (see Table 4.3) remain unmet, job dissatisfaction will result. In contrast, another set of motivation factors must be met in order for there to be job satisfaction. Holtz then gave a 20-item questionnaire, based on the theory, to 31 nursing assistants employed at one long-term-care facility for at least 12 months. The relatively long-term employment was used as an index of relative satisfaction. Hygiene and motivation factors, particularly interpersonal relationships, supervision, achievement, and responsibility were rated as most important in nursing assistant job satisfaction. The nursing assistants viewed their jobs as relevant and important. Interestingly, salary was rated in a lowly sixth position (along with administrative policies and recognition), suggesting that low pay in long-term care may not be a strong disincentive. Job Redesign has also been used as a model for studying organizational issues in long-term care.

Rountree and Deckard (1986), Brannon et al. (1988), Brannon and Bodnar (1988), and Smyer, Brannon, and Cohn (1992) introduced Hackman and Oldham's (1975) Job Redesign to the study of long-term-care management (see Table 4.3). Rountree and Deckard (1986) dispelled the myth that registered nurses and practical nurses in long-term care were a miserably unhappy group. The authors claimed that three psychological states are necessary to achieve desirable goals. First, the work must be meaningful. Second, a feeling of being personally accountable for the work is essential. Third, the worker must receive knowledge of the outcome, whether it be positive or negative. In their study, Rountree and Deckard used the principles of Job Redesign and sent questionnaires to 1,118 professionals in a corporate chain of long-term-care facilities. They received a 94% response rate. Task significance, the degree to which the job has an impact on the lives of others, was ranked higher by long-term-care nurses than by professionals in other settings. The other factors–skill variety, task identity, autonomy, and feedback–were rated roughly equally to those in other settings, leaving the authors to conclude that nursing in long-term care is often rewarding.

Brannon et al. (1988), Brannon and Bodnar (1988), and Smyer, Brannon, and Cohn (1992) applied the principles of Job Redesign to the study of nursing assistants and practical nurses (see Table 4.3). Brannon et al. and Brannon and Bodnar reported on questionnaire data from 21 long-term-care facilities, with 388 nursing assistants and 101 practical nurses participating. The results were as follows:

1. *Skill variety*–Nursing assistants described their work as repetitive and scored lower than the national norms, whereas practical nurses rated variety as high.
2. *Task identity*–Both nursing assistants and practical nurses rated their jobs as directly affecting the whole resident.
3. *Task significance*–Both assistants and practical nurses rated their jobs highly and were well aware of the importance of what they did.

4. *Autonomy*–Nursing assistants have limited autonomy, but rated themselves no lower on this aspect than other laborers, whereas practical nurses recognized higher autonomy in their job.
5. *Feedback*–Nursing assistants and practical nurses, like most workers, received inadequate feedback on their work.

Smyer, Brannon, and Cohn (1992) performed a study to assess the effectiveness of Job Redesign with nursing assistants and practical nurses. Four settings were used and were divided into a control group, a skills-training group only, a Job Redesign group only, and a Skills Training and Job Redesigning group. The Job Redesign incorporated two changes: team nursing approaches and increased nursing assistant involvement in care planning. The results showed that the sites receiving Job Redesign did show a moderate, though not statistically significant, increase in satisfaction. This was primarily due to the increased skill variety scores.

Summary and Critique

Much of the organizational research in long-term-care facilities refutes the perception that all workers are miserably unhappy with their work and pay. Alongside of these findings, however, Barton (1977) and Sbordone and Sterman's (1983) consultative experiences are illustrative. Communication among long-term-care employees is often significantly limited, especially between hierarchies, and this leads to distortions and dissatisfaction. Brannon and her colleagues presented data that support this view, describing the lack of skill variety, autonomy, and supervision nursing assistants receive.

To improve the quality of psychosocial care, the weaknesses of an organizational approach must be addressed. There are two major weaknesses to using solely an organizational intervention. First, as with using only training, an organizational intervention leaves out important skills. Giving nursing assistants more autonomy, for instance, may not lead to much improvement if they are not also given better training on patient-care methods. The second criticism, as stated in an earlier section, is that interventions with long-term-care staff are unlikely to be useful unless they are ongoing. Brief organizational interventions will lead to transitory changes at best.

Long-term-care facilities are a changing industry, full of administrative and personnel changes. Without ongoing involvement by an expert in psychosocial care (and in the organizational methods to accomplish this), gains will not be maintained.

UTILIZING A TEAM APPROACH

A team approach represents an opportunity to combine increased, pertinent, practical training with organizational improvements (particularly in communication and conflict resolution) as a means of improving psychosocial care. Geriatric treatment teams have been fashionable for decades, and the research in this area will be reviewed and followed by the unique approach to long-term-care team functioning that was created and utilized at the Shenandoah Geriatric Treatment Center.

Teams have long been hailed in health care as the best way to deliver care–despite the fact that few methodologically sound studies have been performed on team care (Halstead, 1976). In addition, the experiences of some clinicians and teams are quite sobering (DeSantis, 1983; Bates-Smith and Tsukuda, 1984). Desantis found that team members from a long-term-care facility spent their time vying for influence, rather than focusing on patient goals, and that team meetings were routinely boycotted. Bates-Smith and Tsukuda found that value differences and role confusions too often deter team functioning. These studies are useful in that they illustrate the necessity to plan team interactions and to build team cohesiveness.

Halstead (1976) critically reviewed 25 years of team care in chronic illness. To be counted as a team, the institution simply had to have three members of different disciplines meeting regularly. Ten empirical studies of teams were found. In five studies, patients treated by teams had better functional outcomes, whereas there was no difference between groups in the other five studies. In four studies, patients treated by teams showed less deterioration secondary to disease. Finally, in eight of the ten patient groups treated by teams, team care was more effective in at least one component. Simply by meeting regularly with other disciplines, patient care was modestly improved.

Feiger and Schmitt (1979) studied communication in a long-term-care team and its effects on patient care. Four groups, each treating 30 patients, were created–three with different leaders of the team and one group treated without a team. Videotapes of team meetings were made, and those teams ranking high in collegiality had the best patient outcomes. Lichtenberg, Strzepek, and Zeiss (1990) reported similar findings. By introducing an interdisciplinary team training, collegiality, knowledge, and team attendance all significantly increased compared with a control group.

Descriptive papers continue to advocate for team care in geriatrics (Cole and Campbell, 1986; Abraham et al., 1991). Cole and Campbell stressed occupational therapists' satisfaction with training in team care. Especially useful team skills were active listening, giving constructive feedback to team members, and asserting oneself on a team. Abraham et al. discussed the development and implementation of a team approach to an outpatient geropsychiatric clinic.

A balanced understanding of teams must be developed if they are to succeed in long-term-care facilities. Simply assembling people together on a weekly or biweekly basis does not foster team care, and in fact, is likely to present more problems in long-term care than payoffs. One must understand the process of team functioning, potential problems, and solutions. In the next section, five different papers will be reviewed (see Table 4.4). Each of these authors investigated the process by which teams function.

Models for Understanding Teams

Givens and Simmons (1977) focused on the barriers to team functioning and on the elements necessary for a successful team (Table 4.4). In discussing barriers to team functioning, the authors point out that educational programs are profession-oriented, not team-oriented. As a consequence, professionals know little about other professionals and how they may be of assistance. Role ambiguity on a team is viewed as a second potential barrier. Two professionals may overlap in duties, and some professionals may feel that this presents a conflict, while others may withdraw from fully performing their duties. Authority, power, and status can all be barriers to team functioning. In the medical model, physicians have the highest authority and status. Teams must learn to share authority

TABLE 4.4. Different Models of Understanding Geriatric Health-Care Teams

Author	Focus
1. Given and Simmons (1977)	a. <u>Barriers to team functioning</u>: educational preparation, role ambiguity, authority, power, status, autonomy, personal characteristics. b. <u>Vital elements for a successful team</u>: new communication patterns, authority changes, conflict resolution, administrative support for teams.
2. Liebowitz and DeMuse (1982)	<u>Team Building</u>: teamwork, data collection, long term commitment adminstrative support, team leader support.
3. Brown and Zimberg (1982)	<u>Physical v. Psychosocial care</u>: Value differences, training influences, affect management, patient expectations.
4. Faulkner (1985)	<u>Educational Issues for Teams</u>: Common goals, orientation to aging, team composition, problem solving, decision making, team support.
5. Qualls and Czirr (1988)	<u>Professional Models</u>: Logic of assessments, focus of professional efforts, locus of responsibility, pace of action. <u>Team Models</u>: Focus of group attention, expectation about decision making, beliefs about interdisciplinary dependence.

according to the expertise required in a situation. Teams can also threaten the autonomy that physicians or head nurses feel. Finally, differing personal characteristics such as age, sex, values, etc., may be barriers to good team functioning.

Givens and Simmons also focused their attention on elements vital for an interdisciplinary team. They ranked both the selection of appropriate members and the provision of time designated for developing working relationships as a high priority. The focus of teams should be on the services to be delivered. First, new professional interaction patterns are encouraged. Each professional learns to recognize the point at which other disciplines need to be brought in. Cooperation must replace competition, and communication must be informal as well as formal, flexible, and open. Acts of leadership from all members are vital to team functioning; as a result, authority and status has to change. Conflict resolution is taught and practiced. Most team conflict revolves around how to pursue treatment and is not focused on the treatment goal(s). Finally, the institutional management must support team formation. In sum, a period of reeducation and work is necessary so that a group can become a team.

Liebowitz and DeMeuse (1982) approached team building from a corporate, organizational perspective. Much of their philosophy can be directly translated to geriatric care (Table 4.4). They described two forces leading to the use of a team: (1) teams improve the ability of an organization to change and (2) the work revolves around interdependencies among organizational members. Team building, they stated, is a long-term, data-based intervention in which groups learn to increase teamwork skills. The authors outlined five necessary conditions for successful team building. Teamwork must be valued, and a long-term commitment is necessary. Formal data collection on team problems and solutions are required, as is the active support of senior management and the support of the team leader. In their review of team building, they cited its advantages: increased productivity, decreased turnover, increased employee satisfaction, and increased team effectiveness.

Brown and Zimberg (1982) compared the professional value differences found in those physicians who focused mainly on medical practices with those professionals focused mainly on psychological practice (Table 4.4). The authors pursued this inquiry to shed light on why difficulties persisted in integrating physical and psychological practices. Value differences were cited as one area causing conflict. In medical practice, one approaches a problem by ruling out disease, whereas psychological practice rules in all aspects of emotional functioning. Medical practice is action-oriented, and psychological treatment is relatively slower. Medical practitioners act in an executive capacity, feeling responsible for all decisions. In contrast, those with a psychological practice seek a partnership with their patients and take the necessary time to create a trusting relationship. Brown and Zimberg cite training influences as another factor in the difficulty of integrative care. Medical schools' focus on the body makes psychological processes seem superficial. In addition, affect is managed differently by different practitioners. Medical practice requires that affect be isolated and kept from interfering with a procedure, whereas in a psychological practice, affect is to be utilized in treatment. Brown and Zimberg caution that considerable effort must be made to achieve integrated care.

Faulkner (1985) acknowledged the barriers to geriatric team care but offered suggestions on how to educate interdisciplinary teams (Table 4.4). Similar to the other authors reviewed here, Faulkner observed that strong professional orientation and a lack of interdisciplinary vocabulary were major barriers to effective team care. To improve this, she offered six steps. First, common goals are identified. For example, supported autonomy, continuous treatment of chronic illness, and encouraging emotional growth were offered as interdisciplinary goals. Second, team members are oriented to aging and the aged. Third, they must recognize both ageism (i.e., seeing aging only as problems) and the unique aspects and conflicts of aging (e.g., to always sustain life). Fourth, teams must be expanded to include physicians, nurses, psychologists, social workers, nutritionists, and rehabilitation therapists. Fifth, teams need to recognize two tracks of problem solving. The first track is the medical-health-centered (patient treatment), and the second is the interpersonal dynamics of the team. Problem solving is to be accomplished in both areas. Sixth, Faulkner echoes others in recognizing the need for interdisciplinary decision making and concluding that the support teams may prevent burnout.

Qualls and Czirr (1988) focus on the problems noted during their long experience with an interdisciplinary training program (Table 4.4). They, similar to Brown and Zimberg, focused on differing professional models of functioning. Their logic of assessment mirrored Brown and Zimberg's conceptualization of ruling out problems to identify one cause, versus ruling in problems to look at interactions. The professional-effort continuum found an acute medical focus at one extreme and social issues at the other. Professional responsibility was described as ranging from occupying the role of the executive (with the patient following orders) to viewing the professional as a consultant and the patient as the decision maker. Finally, the pace of action was divided up to look at immediate results versus paced evaluation and treatment.

The authors also focused on the group process among the interdisciplinary team members. Again, using a continuum to describe extremes, Qualls and Czirr addressed how the group spent its time (quick decisions with only factual data versus a focus on process issues); decision making models (one person making all decisions versus group consensus); and beliefs about interdisciplinary dependence (autonomy versus no responsibility). The authors stressed the importance of professionals learning more about other disciplines and of acquiring basic teamwork skills.

The five studies reviewed above all echoed the same important themes: (1) teams are created through hard work and education and not by simply assembling professionals together; (2) conflict is normal on teams, and conflict resolution is an integral part of team functioning; (3) teams must be viewed as a long-term solution and have the support of both upper management and the team leader (physician); and (4) professionals can strive to learn more about the work of their colleagues. Teams hold great promise for long-term care. First, they can be used to improve communication and coordinate treatment among all professionals. Second, in the team context and with the proper team development or team training, nursing assistants and practical nurses can be effectively incorporated into the team, thereby providing tremendous knowledge about current patient treatments. Third, through the team approach, nursing assistants and practical nurses can receive much needed training, which will help them effectively resolve organizational issues. The next section will describe the experience of building an interdisciplinary team at the Shenandoah Geriatric Treatment Center.

A Team-Building Approach

As with most long-term-care facilities, most of the Center's nursing assistants and practical nurses were rarely seen in the team meetings. When they did attend, they did not speak unless spoken to. Team meetings often got bogged down and took hours to complete, with no clear purpose. Dissatisfaction was rampant. As a result, a small group of professionals was charged with assessing the approach of the eight teams and making recommendations for improvement. An organizational approach was used, similar to that used by Sbordone and Sterman (1983) and Liebowitz and DeMeuse (1982). Data were collected by observing each team twice and by interviewing team members, most of the nursing assistants, and licensed practical nurses on the units.

The findings revealed three major trends: (1) attendance was spotty among all team members, reflecting disorganization and dissatisfaction on the team; (2) the nursing assistants and licensed practical nurses felt shut out and disrespected; and (3) team meetings were too time-consuming, often lasting as long as three hours to discuss five to seven patients. As a result of this assessment, a team-building approach utilizing organizational changes and instituting new training was begun. Training consisted of a week of didactic lectures. These lectures were taped so that all of the staff not in attendance, and those who worked on different shifts, could view the presentations. Topics such as behavior management, psychotropic medication usage, dementia, medical recordkeeping, assertiveness in the work place, and a psychosocial nursing approach were presented.

The newly constituted teams met to define their purpose and to enlarge the team to include nursing assistants and licensed practical nurses. It was decided to categorize the patient concerns into three areas: behavior problems, social needs, and medical problems. The first task at each meeting was to describe what difficulties the patient was presenting. These included such things as agitation, hostility, withdrawal, combativeness, wandering, and crying spells. Problems were defined by specific behavioral descriptive terms rather than broad categorical ones (e.g., "resistive," "unmotivated"). Practical treatment plans were then developed, as was a method for assessing the effectiveness of the plan. Team input, especially from the nursing assistants and practical nurses, and consensus from the nursing staff was reached before plans were written by the psychologists. Plans were focused on reducing two common errors made in long-term-care facilities: (1) overreliance on punishment and (2) rewarding undesirable behaviors. It was explained that to change a behavior, one must replace it with a new behavior through the use of positive reinforcement.

The progress of teams was reevaluated in six months. Although their attendance at meetings was good, nursing assistants and practical nurses still felt intimidated and participated very little. Professionals from different disciplines continued to ignore one another. One simple behavioral intervention to help a patient finish his meal and not hoard food, for example, was never followed by the nursing assistant staff. When asked about this confidentially, they expressed pessimism about the plan's effectiveness; they said that following the plan would be giving this patient undue "extra attention." These concerns contributed heavily to sabotaging the plan. On another team, a conflict about a patient's clothes raged on. The social services staff wanted to take some patients shopping for new clothes. The nursing assistant staff objected, stating that these patients ripped all their clothes. However, the social services workers continued to buy new clothes, the patients continued to rip them, and the nursing assistants continued to feel frustrated. It was clear that gaps remained in this team approach.

In her insightful article, Dawes (1981) stated that including nursing assistants on teams was only useful if nursing assistants received training in team communication skills and if all professions explored one another's roles and prejudices about their colleagues. My colleague, Dr. Deborah Strzepek, suggested that the Veterans' Administration's Interdisciplinary Team Training in Geriatrics program (ITTG) be adapted to long-term care. Since a new dementia program was opening, it was decided that the ITTG model be used. After initially presenting 12 weekly sessions (and, later, two six-session refresher series), the use of ITTG in long-term care appears well justified.

History of ITTG

The Interdisciplinary Team Training in Geriatrics was originated by the Office of Academic Affairs in the Veterans' Administration in 1979. ITTG is a systematic educational program designed to include didactic and clinical instruction for VA faculty practitioners and affiliated students from three or more health professions, such as physicians, nurses, psychologists, social workers, etc. The ITTG provides a structured approach to the delivery of health services by emphasizing the knowledge and skills needed to work in an interactive group. In addition, the program promotes an understanding of the roles and functions of other members of the team and how their collaborative contributions influence both the delivery and outcome of patient care.

Each of the 12 ITTG sites is charged with developing and evaluating their own programs for implementing the general ITTG philosophy. At the Palo Alto (Calif.) VA Medical Center, which served as the model for the program instituted at the Shenandoah Geriatric Treatment Center, ITTG emphasizes the following topics in the educational program: team theory; understanding the skills and training of each profession on the team; increasing knowledge about the special problems of geriatric patients (and the need for diverse skills to address them); developing a model of constructive disagreement among team members; and developing skills for negotiating resolution when there is disagreement.

Initial Training

The initial 12-session training was divided into two modules: a focus on teams and team communication and on training sessions to improve psychosocial care (see Table 4.5). In Table 4.5, an outline of each training session is presented. Here, specific methods will be discussed. In the first session, a definition of an interdisciplinary team was explored. The distinction between multi- and interdisciplinary teams helps clarify some of the primary sources of resistance to implementing ITTG that will be discussed later. In multidisciplinary teams, members come from a mix of health and social-welfare professions. They may share a common work site, but individual professional identities are more important than the

TABLE 4.5. Interdisciplinary Team Training for Long-Term-Care Facilities

<u>Module 1:</u> Focusing efforts on models of team functioning and developing communications on a team.

1. Understanding the differences in types of teams
   a. Inter v. Multi disciplinary
   b. Stages of team development
   c. Benefits of a cohesive team
2. Understanding one's own discipline and that of others
   a. Biomedical v. psychosocial model
   b. How operating from different models often causes conflict.
3. Communication Skills
   a. How to use active listening at a team conference
   b. How to use assertive statements at a team conference
4. Conflict Resolution (2 sessions)
   a. Learn the four steps to resolving conflict
   b. Become aware of what typically impedes conflict resolution
5. Stress and Burnout in Long Term Care
   a. Learning time management
   b. Utilizing relaxation techniques

<u>Module 2:</u> Training sessions to improve psychosocial interactions with patients.

1. Transition into long term care
   a. How to assist patients in making successful transition
   b. Common errors when intervening with those in transition
2. Dementia
   a. Behavioral characteristics of demented patients
   b. Use of reassurance and redirection to communicate with troubled patients
3. Depression
   a. Identifying symptoms of depression
   b. Behavioral and pharmacological therapies
4. Neuropsychology of dementia
   a. 5 areas of cognitive functioning
   b. Compensatory strategies
5. Competency
   a. Legal v. clinical issue
   b. Competency for specific areas not a generalized judgement
6. Working with families
   a. Identifying stages of caregiving
   b. Identifying common problems among caregivers

team identity. Members work independently and do not implement a common plan; however, they may share information about their individual efforts and may consult with each other. It is a hierarchical structure, with the highest-ranking professional or person (who is appointed by the administration) generally assuming the leadership role. Members do not attend to the interactional process, because the team is not the primary vehicle for service delivery.

As with the multidisciplinary team, members on an interdisciplinary team come from a mix of professions. But this team has a collective identity that is more important than the individual professional status of each member. Team members share common goals, collaborate, and work interdependently in planning, problem solving, decision making, implementation, and evaluation. It is a nonhierarchical structure, with all members sharing the right and responsibility for assuming leadership functions as needed to facilitate team progress. Each member's voice is considered to be of equal value. Because such interdependent work requires smooth functioning among team members, it also requires attention to the team's internal interactional processes. Members understand that effective team functioning does not just happen. Communication, role negotiation, and other critical skills are practiced.

The stages of team development were also explored. The four stages of team development–forming, storming, norming, and performing–were outlined. When groups form, there is discomfort and stiffness. Politeness dominates early team conferences, leading to slightly increased cohesiveness. Eventually, the group begins to experience conflict (storming). Team conflict is inevitable and normal, so the team must be able to resolve conflicts appropriately. When this is done, cohesiveness increases and groups begin norming. That is, they develop a sense of how they work and what issues they can safely address. Finally, in the performing stage, the team emits a sense of belongingness and deep commitment and is well focused on their task.

The second session is focused on understanding one's own model of training, sharing this understanding, and listening to others share theirs (Table 4.5). Team members must learn about their colleagues' training and model for functioning (refer to Brown and

Zimberg, 1982; Qualls and Czirr, 1988). To do so, each team member filled out the following questions and presented their responses:

1. List four functions held by members of your profession.
2. List your profession's major contribution to health care.
3. What additional roles do you think others in your profession should have?
4. What role do you want to perform on the unit?
5. Describe the educational requirements for your profession.

This exercise brought out two major findings. First, each team member, by sharing his/her views, also shared his/her commitment to the elderly. This gave each member a common bond. Second, by sharing their views, nursing assistants put to rest the idea that they had no specific model of training. In fact, they were very much attuned to the medical, biological model. It was then reviewed how different models lead to conflict in treatment approaches.

Communication skills, required for teams to work well, was the focus of the third session (Table 4.5). Active listening and using an assertiveness approach were stressed. Open-ended questioning, reflecting content and feelings, are basic active-listening skills. Didactics, demonstration, and observed practice were used to get team members to identify how they could use these techniques and then actually implement them.

The dos and don'ts of assertiveness were also reviewed and practiced. The don'ts include: blaming, name calling, attributing personality traits, bringing up multiple issues, threatening, overgeneralizing or being vague, and presenting the solution in the same breath as the complaint. Team members often convince themselves not to bring up issues, because they think they will be rejected, others will be angry with them, they will be ignored, they will get reprimanded, or receive a bad evaluation. Making assertive statements–saying what one is feeling by announcing one's thoughts simply and clearly–was emphasized. A typical assertive statement is: "When you do X in situation Y, I feel Z." For example, when a team member is often late, an assertive statement would be: "When you show up late consistently, I feel frustrated." Five vignettes were presented, and assertive statements were generated by the team. Following this, supervised role plays were implemented.

Conflict resolution was presented over the course of two sessions (Table 4.5). Four steps for resolving conflict were presented. They are: (1) separate the people from the problem; (2) focus on goals, not on positions; (3) generate a variety of possibilities (brainstorming) before deciding what to do; and (4) the result should be based, and later evaluated, on some objective standard. Team conflicts often occur between the same individuals over a variety of issues. These individuals may be operating from different models of functioning, and so they routinely view things differently. Before long, however, these conflicts become personal confrontations. Thus, it is important to first step back and separate the problem from the person with whom you are in disagreement.

Focusing on goals and not positions is a second step toward deescalating the emotional tug of war between team members. Too often, teams argue over positions (i.e., the means of doing something, the "how to") before they have ever clarified the desired outcome. Thus, the second step in conflict resolution is focusing on goals. This serves to take the focus off the team members' ways of doing things and to put the emphasis on the patient's needs.

Generating a variety of options (brainstorming) is necessary for many of the complex problems in long-term care, and is the next step of conflict resolution. In brainstorming, all possible solutions are encouraged. A facilitator should be chosen for the brainstorming session. The atmosphere should be informal, and there must be no criticism or evaluative comments on any of the ideas presented. All ideas should be recorded.

The last step in resolving conflict is choosing a solution that is based on some objective standard. To achieve this, the more promising ideas from the brainstorming session should be considered first. When all agree to a particular plan, it is important to be certain that it is one that can be quantitatively measured and its success evaluated.

Six months later, refresher sessions were held. These were mostly for the nursing assistants and practical nurses. The refresher sessions focused on practical applications of assertive communication and conflict resolution. The following are examples of how the team was functioning in new and better ways. Staff became much more comfortable in making suggestions outside their disciplines.

For instance, one nursing assistant, who at one time had been wheelchair-bound herself, offered the physician a useful suggestion for the treatment of a wheelchair-bound patient. Staff became more comfortable, with more members becoming active participants rather than always deferring to professional staff. It became much more common, for instance, for aides to disagree with a physician or to slow down a discussion if they felt professional staff members were railroading their own personal opinions without sufficient input from other team members. In one particularly heated discussion, the nursing assistants finally persuaded the physician that he was over-medicating a patient. Before ITTG, they would have simply griped about this behind his back. They were able to do this by using some of the skills they learned in training, such as, "I feel uncomfortable that the suggestion that Mrs. T. is overmedicated was just dropped with no input from other team members."

ITTG members also became more adept at identifying roots of conflict (e.g., those evolving out of differences in professional models), and they also became more comfortable in negotiating conflict. For example, nursing staff who believed it was their job to make sure patients were well groomed wanted the psychologist to develop a treatment plan to stop a demented male from dressing in multiple layers of clothing. In the psychologist's view, the struggle and distress this intervention would cause the patient did not warrant the effort. When it was pointed out that his odd dress posed no health problem, and that he was so skinny that his multiple layers of clothing were not readily apparent and thus did him no social harm, this issue did not become a power struggle between disciplines.

Lichtenberg, Strzepek, and Zeiss (1990) published their findings that indicated the effectiveness of ITTG in long-term care. Using only a posttest, the group undergoing the ITTG process scored significantly better than a matched control group. In addition, attendance at team meetings increased by 60% for the four months subsequent to the intervention (and remained at that level at an 18-month followup). Two case studies highlight the usefulness of ITTG.

Mrs. K. Mrs. K. grew up in the rural Midwest, where her father was a farmer. She was the eldest of three children. She described her childhood as chaotic and fun, telling story after story of how her father was a local clown. Hilarious as many of the stories appeared, Mrs. K. related a life with an irresponsible, alcoholic father who failed to provide for the family's security and safety needs. After graduating from high school, Mrs. K. moved to the city. While living with an aunt, she worked in a grocery store. Soon, she met a soldier and married him during wartime. The couple later had three children. Her husband became a colonel, and she worked as a real estate agent. In fact, she sold many properties and was soon earning more money than her husband.

During her forties, Mrs. K. began to display symptoms of alcoholism. She was arrested often for Driving While Intoxicated, and she began engaging in violent fights with her husband. He, too, was abusing alcohol. She was hospitalized in several alcohol-treatment programs but never finished a single one. Her husband died in his fifties. Mrs. K. drank alcohol more and more. She developed severe physical problems. A seizure disorder cropped up during an abrupt alcohol withdrawal. This was followed by a large right middle cerebral artery infarct, which caused left hemiparesis. In addition, Mrs. K. developed chronic bronchitis and obstructive pulmonary disease.

A neuropsychological assessment revealed many cognitive strengths. Mrs. K. displayed intact attentional skills and good verbal-recall memory abilities. Visuospatial deficits were noted, consistent with her stroke. Mrs. K. was reporting moderate depression, with complaints of boredom, hopelessness, helplessness, and feeling blue. Depression appeared highly related to her physical decline. Behaviorally, Mrs. K. was extremely negativistic, refusing psychological treatment and refusing to participate in her self-care. She was verbally abusive to the nursing assistants if they did not act upon her requests immediately. As a result, she was much feared and disliked by the nursing assistant staff. Her children were not in contact with her and refused to answer her calls. Mrs. K.'s support needs were clearly in the area of physical functioning; she needed considerable assistance with ADL tasks. Autonomy needs were determined to be crucial, so she would have a sense of personal control over her environment and relationships.

Problems were seen in the areas of physical, interpersonal, and family functioning. She had the physical capabilities to participate more in her ADL tasks. Second, she had the cognitive abilities to monitor her interpersonal behavior and reduce her verbal abusiveness. Third, she had the cognitive abilities and emotional desire to be more involved with her family. After each discipline performed its evaluation, the team met and created a behavioral contract, which was submitted to Mrs. K. It specified staff and patient responsibilities, providing both groups with some personal control. The plan included the following:

1. Patient will propel self in wheelchair.
2. Staff to take patient to toilet upon request, help transfer her to the commode, and when she is finished, help her back into the chair.
3. Tissues, glasses, and lip balm will be accessible to patient in her dresser.
4. Bed will be made according to patient specifications.
5. When patient becomes verbally hostile, staff will cease providing care, and then return ten minutes later to resume care.
6. When patient throws items on floor (tissues, magazines, etc.), she will pick them up.
7. Patient will set own schedule for waking and dressing.

The mental-health worker began to contact Mrs. K.'s children, keeping them abreast of their mother's functioning. In time, they became more involved in her life, helping her track her finances and visiting on a regular, though infrequent, basis. Mrs K. significantly improved her self-care involvement and reduced her verbal abusiveness.

This case highlights the importance of using a true team approach in treatment. The team was unified and the responsibility for care was placed back in Mrs. K's hands. She was given control over her daily schedule, and it was her behavior that determined the staff help she received. For example, her verbal abusiveness would prevent her from getting helped into bed to take a nap, rather than the staff imposing a regimented schedule. The behavioral contract also provided reassurance that her support needs, particularly for physical care, would be met.

Mrs. M. At the age of seven, Mrs. M. was abandoned by her parents and went to live with an aunt who severely abused her, often banging Mrs. M.'s head against the wall. As a teenager, Mrs. M. married a man 20 years her senior. He beat her regularly, often striking her about the head. At age 30 damage to her brain was causing a burning sensation, as well as numbness, weakness, pain, and depression. Mrs. M. was given an intellectual assessment, and her score placed her in the range of mild mental retardation. Her verbal skills were better than visuospatial skills, and her attention was a strength while problem solving was a prominent deficit. Mrs. M., a 65-year-old married homemaker, was brought to long-term care due to severe agitation and crying. She exhibited long periods of yelling at others and accusing them of harming her. She was diagnosed with the psychiatric diagnosis of an organic mood syndrome, indicating brain damage that was not specified as to location.

On the unit, Mrs. M. complained constantly of staff abuse. She slept poorly, screamed often, and struck out and hit other patients. The staff, trying desperately to appease her, were giving in to her outrageous requests of receiving three whirlpool baths per day. Inadvertently, the staff was rewarding her undesirable outbursts. It was at this point that the nursing assistants brought Mrs. M.'s problems to the attention of the team. Thus, the strategy was to reduce her outburst and to increase her prosocial behavior.

The team met after a psychological consultation was completed and agreed to institute a behavioral technique known as Differential Reinforcement of Other Behaviors (DRO). The target behaviors of loud yelling, crying, or hitting were selected. Initially, Mrs. M. had the opportunity to earn small rewards (e.g., coffee, phone call to family, manicure) in three one-hour periods each day. If she earned 13 small rewards in one week, she was given a large reward (e.g., trip to town, trip to snack bar); during the next week, the times increased by 15 minutes, thus demanding more from Mrs. M., but using the same type of reward system. At all times Mrs. M. screamed or hit others, she was placed in time-out for 30 minutes. Her behavior steadily improved. By six months, she reduced her screaming by 50% and her hitting by 80%. By 12 months, she no longer hit anyone and her screaming was rare.

Ten months into the plan, however, following an acute illness, Mrs. M. began screaming and crying–the plan was no longer working. The rewards had lost their potency, and observation revealed that arguing with staff on the way to time-out was now rewarding. The nursing assistants, armed with quantitative data, asked for a new approach. It was this direct feedback from the nursing assistants to the psychologist that led to a new plan.

Soon thereafter, a plan calling for non-exclusionary time-out was introduced. Mrs. M. was given a corsage to wear when she was calm and quiet. When the corsage was on, she received verbal praise and social reinforcers. When Mrs. M. began to yell, curse, or accuse others, the corsage was taken and Mrs. M. was ignored and excluded from all activities. Every 15 minutes, the staff would check to see if Mrs. M. was quiet, and if she was, she received her corsage. The only time the care plan was to be interrupted was for medical reasons or emergencies. The plan did not show much promise during its first four months. However, gains were fast in coming after that period. Mrs. M. went two weeks without losing the corsage. Unfortunately, the day she did yell it lasted much of the day. At the next team meeting, the licensed practical nurse asked that the plan be dropped because it was not working. Her impression was clouded by the sheer awful experience of that one day. The quantitative data showed that the plan was working and, so, it was retained. During the next 60 days, Mrs. M. lost her corsage only once, and then only briefly.

This case highlights several points. First, it shows the importance of having staff consensus before embarking on an ambitituous plan, because success comes slowly. Second, no plan works forever. Teams must be flexible in their treatment efforts. Third, quantitative data must be obtained to evaluate treatment. In this case, quantitative data identified when the plan was working and when it was no longer useful, whereas qualitative data and staff perceptions were vulnerable to bias and false conclusions. Finally, this case demonstrates that teams can positively impact even the most difficult of problems.

ITTG: A Cautionary Note

When ITTG was first brought to him, the top administrator of clinical services was very skeptical. He firmly believed that the interdisciplinary method was a way for team members to avoid specific responsibilities. In addition, staff at all levels were skeptical of the approach. Nursing assistants worried that they would be punished for voicing their opinions, and registered nurses worried that their authority would be undermined. At times, they were right. Some of the nursing assistants' fears came true and they were criticized for being "too outspoken." Also, some gentle persuasion and reminding needed to be done with the registered nurses and physicians. Over time, however, ITTG became a cornerstone of the dementia unit and an approach valued by all.

REFERENCES

Abraham, I.L., Thompson-Heisterman, A.A., Harrington, D.P., Smullen, D.E., Onega, L.L., Droney, E.G., Westerman, P.S., Manning, C.A., and Lichtenberg, P.A. (1991). Outpatient Psychogeriatric Nursing Services: An Integrative Model. *Archives of Psychiatric Nursing, 5*, 151-164.

Almquist, E., and Bates, D. (1980). Training Program for Nursing Assistants and LPNs in Nursing Homes. *Journal of Gerontological Nursing, 6*, 623-627.

Baltes, M.M. (1983). The Etiology and Maintenance of Dependency in the Elderly: Three Phases of Operant Research. *Behavior Therapy, 19*, 301-319.

Barton, R. (1977). Communication in the Nursing Home: Concepts and Issues. *Nursing Homes*, 8-13.

Bates-Smith, K., and Tsukuda, R.A. (1984). Problems of an Interdisciplinary Training Team. *Clinical Gerontologist, 3*, 66-68.

Brannon, D., and Bodnar, J. (1988). The Primary Caregivers: Aides and LPNs. In M. Smyer and M. Cohn (Eds.) *Mental Health Consultation in Nursing Homes*. New York University Press: New York. 192-212.

Brannon, D., Smyer, M.A., Cohn, M.D., Borchardt, L., Landry, J.A., Jay, G.M., Garfein, A.J., Malonebeach, E., and Walls, C. (1988). A Job Diagnostic Survey of Nursing Home Caregivers: Implications for Job Redesign. *Gerontologist, 28*, 246-252.

Brown, H.N., and Zimberg, N.E. (1982). Difficulties in the Integration of Psychological and Medical Practices. *American Journal of Psychiatry, 139*, 1576-1580.

Burgio, L.D., and Burgio, K.L. (1990). Institutional Staff Training and Management: A Review of the Literature and a Model for Geriatric, Long-Term-Care Facilities. *International Journal on Aging and Human Development, 30*, 287-302.

Burgio, L.D., Whitman, T.L., and Reid, D.H. (1983). A Participative Management Approach for Improving Direct-Care Staff Performance in an Institutional Setting. *Journal of Applied Behavior Analysis, 16*, 37-53.

Burgio, L.D., Engel, B.T., Hawkins, A., McCormick, K., and Scheve, A. (1990). Descriptive Analysis of Nursing Staff Behaviors in a Teaching Nursing Home: Differences Among NAs, LPNs, and RNs. *Gerontologist, 30*, 107-112.

Caston, R.J. (1983). The Role of Education and Health Care Delivery Structure in Quality of Nursing Care for Mentally Ill Patients in Nursing Homes. *Educational Gerontology, 9,* 425-433.

Chartock, P., Nevins, A., Rzetelny, H., and Gilberto, P. (1988). A Mental Health Training Program in Nursing Homes. *The Gerontologist, 28,* 503-507.

Cohn, M.D., Horgas, A.L., and Marsiske, M. (1990). Behavior Management Training for Nurse Aides: Is it Effective? *Journal of Gerontological Nursing, 16,* 21-24.

Cohn, M.D., Smyer, M.A., Garfein, A.J., Droogas, A., and Malonebeach, E.E. (1987). Perceptions of Mental Health Training in Nursing Homes: Congruence Among Administrators and Nurse's Aides. *Journal of Long Term Care Administration, Summer,* 20-25.

Cole, K.D., and Campbell, L.J. (1986). Interdisciplinary Team Training for Occupational Therapists. *Physical and Occupational Therapy in Geriatrics, 4,* 69-74.

Dawes, P.L. (1981). The Nurses' Aide and the Team Approach in the Nursing Home. *Journal of Geriatric Psychiatry, 14,* 265-277.

DeSantis, G. (1983). From Teams to Hierarchy: A Short-Lived Innovation in a Hospital for the Elderly. *Social Science Medicine, 17,* 1613-1618.

Faulkner, A.O. (1985). Interdisciplinary Health Care Teams: An Educational Approach to Improvement of Health Care for the Aged. *Gerontology and Geriatrics Education, 5,* 29-39.

Feiger, S.M., and Schmitt, M. (1979). Collegiality in Interdisciplinary Health Teams: Its Measurement and Its Effects. *Social Science Medicine, 13,* 217-229.

Givens, B., and Simmons, S. (1977). The Interdisciplinary Health Care Team: Fact or Fiction? *Nursing Forum, 26,* 165-184.

Guy, D.W., and Morice, H.O. (1985). A Comparative Analysis of Behavior Management in the Nursing Home. *Clinical Gerontologist, 4,* 11-17.

Hackman, J., and Oldham, G. (1975). Development of the Job Diagnostic Survey. *Journal of Applied Psychology, 60,* 159-170.

Halstead, L.S. (1976). Team Care in Chronic Illness: A Critical Review of the Literature of the Past 25 Years. *Archives of Physical Medicine and Rehabilitation, 57,* 507-511.

Holtz, G.A. (1982). Nurses' Aides in Nursing Homes: Why Are They Satisfied? *Journal of Gerontological Nursing, 8,* 265-271.

Kahana, E.F., and Kiyak, H.A. (1984). Attitudes and Behavior of Staff in Facilities for the Aged. *Research on Aging, 6,* 395-416.

Kasteler, J.M., Ford, M.H., White, M.A., and Carruth, M.L. (1979). Personnel Turnover: A Major Problem for Nursing Homes. *Nursing Homes, 28,* 20-27.

Lebray, P.R. (1979). Geropsychology in Long-Term Care Settings. *Professional Psychology, 10,* 475-484.

Lichtenberg, P., Strzepek, D., and Zeiss, A. (1990). Bringing Psychiatric Aides into the Treatment Team: An Application of the Veterans Administration's ITTG Model. *Gerontology and Geriatrics Education, 10,* 63-73.

Liebowitz, S., and Demeuse, K.P. (1982). The Application of Team Building. *Human Relations, 35*, 1-18.

Mallya, A., and Fitz, D. (1987). A Psychogeriatric Rehabilitation Program in Long Term Care Facilities. *The Gerontologist, 27*, 747-751.

Meunier, G.F., and Holmes, T.R. (1987). Measuring the Behavioral Knowledge of Nursing Home Employees. *Clinical Gerontologist, 6*, 11-17.

Nigl, A.J., and Jackson, B. (1981). A Behavior Management Program to Increase Social Responses in Psychogeriatric Patients. *Journal of the American Geriatrics Society, 29*, 92-95.

Patterson, R.D., and Gurian, B.S. (1976). Long-Term Effects of a Nursing Home Education Project. *Gerontologist, 16*, 65-68.

Qualls, S.H., and Czirr, R. (1988). Geriatric Health Teams: Classifying Models of Professional and Team Functioning. *The Gerontologist, 28*, 372-376.

Reagan, J. (1986). Management of Nurse's Aides in Long-Term Care Settings. *Journal of Long Term Care Administration, 14*, 9-14.

Rountree, B.H., and Deckard, G.J. (1986). Nursing in Long-Term Care: Dispelling a Myth. *Journal of Long Term Care Administration, 14*, 15-19.

Sbordone, R.J., and Sterman, L.T. (1983). The Psychologist as a Consultant in a Nursing Home: Effect on Staff Morale and Turnover. *Professional Psychology, 14*, 240-250.

Schwartz, A. (1974). Staff Development and Morale Building in Nursing Homes. *Gerontologist, 14*, 50-54.

Smith, H.L., Discenza, R., and Saxberg, B.O. (1978). Administering Long-Term Care Services: A Decision-Making Perspective. *The Gerontologist, 18*, 159-166.

Smyer, M., Cohn, M., and Brannon, D. (1988). *Mental Health Consultation in Nursing Homes*. New York University Press: New York.

Smyer, M., Brannon, D. and Cohn, M. (1992). Improving Nursing Home Care Through Training and Job Redesign. *Gerontologist, 32*, 327-333.

Smyer, M.A. (1989). Nursing Homes as a Setting for Psychological Practice. *American Psychologist, 44*, 1307-1314.

Spore, D.L., Smyer, M.A., and Cohn, M.D. (1991). Assessing Nursing Assistants' Knowledge of Behavioral Approaches to Mental Health Problems. *The Gerontologist, 31*, 309-317.

Stein, S., Linn, M.W., and Stein, E. (1986). The Relationship Between Nursing Home Residents' Perceptions of Nursing Staff and Quality of Nursing Home Care. *Journal of Physical and Occupational Therapy, 4*, 143-156.

Waxman, H.M., Carner, E.A., and Berkenstock, G. (1984). Job Turnover and Job Satisfaction Among Nursing Home Aides. *The Gerontologist, 24*, 503-509.

Chapter 5

The Role of Paraprofessional Staff in Psychological Practice

The use of paraprofessionals in the treatment of psychosocial problems was fueled in the 1960s and 1970s by an increased demand for services and by a chronic shortage of professionals (Brown, 1974; Christensen, Miller, and Munoz, 1978). This chapter will review the research on the use of paraprofessionals, emphasizing their usage with the elderly, and highlighting efforts to use paraprofessionals in long-term care. This review will be followed by an in-depth discussion of how to utilize a paraprofessional in a mental-health worker role. Criteria for selecting and training paraprofessionals–as well as supervision structure and case studies–will be presented.

Paraprofessionals' roles have been defined differently by different authors (Karlsruher, 1974). Christensen, Miller, and Munoz (1978) defined the role as one who works beside or alongside of professionals, whereas Moffic et al. (1984) defined the role as a category of mental-health personnel who are identified with a treatment team and are not identified with any of the core disciplines. All authors agree that paraprofessionals have an educational level below a master's degree. Prominent roles for paraprofessionals have included programs for inpatient and outpatient mental health and for child and adolescent education programs.

Several reviews evaluating the effectiveness of paraprofessionals have repeatedly found that paraprofessionals produce effective results (Balch and Solomon, 1976; Brown, 1974; Durlak, 1979; Karlsruher, 1974). Durlak (1979) reviewed 42 studies with respect to outcome and adequacy of design. Paraprofessionals came from four major categories: individual and group psychotherapy, college students, crisis intervention, and specific target problems. Two overall conclusions were reached. First, the experimental quality of the studies reviewed equalled outcome research in other clinical areas. That is, although studies on paraprofessional effectiveness had major methodological flaws, the data was no more or less flawed than were studies on the treatment effectiveness by professionals. Second, convergent evidence provided support that paraprofessionals achieve clinical outcomes equal to professionals, especially in those efforts directed at specific target problems. Durlak also noted the lack of information on the supervisory process between professionals and paraprofessionals. Other major review articles supported Durlak's conclusions.

Brown (1974) stated that studies of paraprofessionals' effectiveness are fraught with methodological problems and that less than 25% of reports (1) compared experimental and control samples, (2) used both pre- and post-assessment, or (3) employed objective criteria. Nevertheless, Brown concurred with Durlak, stating that there was solid evidence of paraprofessional effectiveness. Brown went further and speculated that the selection of paraprofessionals with a high capacity for empathy and warmth was greatly responsible for their effectiveness. Karlsruher's review (1974) focused solely on psychotheraputic effectiveness of paraprofessionals, and it was in general agreement with Brown's. He tied paraprofessional effectiveness to the supervision obtained from professionals, noting that supervised paraprofessionals were rated as more empathic than unsupervised paraprofessionals. Other reviews studied specific paraprofessional interventions.

Balch and Solomon (1976) focused their review solely on paraprofessional effectiveness in using behavioral management techniques. The paraprofessionals reviewed included psychiatric aides, nurses, college students, and community workers. Overall, the authors found general support for the use of paraprofessionals as behavioral modifiers. Methodological flaws, however, and inconsistencies between the studies made any definite conclusions impossible (e.g., lack of control groups and lack of control for experimenter bias). Further, Balch and Solomon raised the question of what the length and nature of paraprofessional training should be. Christensen, Miller, and Munoz (1978) stated that training should include general instruction, rehearsal, specific instruction, and then continued supervision. The major findings of the review papers cited above are summarized in Table 5.1.

Marks, Connolly, and Hallam (1973) provided an example of an impressive usage of paraprofessionals. Five nurses were given training (i.e., seminars, case discussions, videotaped demonstration, and supervised practice) in treating phobic patients. Out of 115 patients screened by a psychiatrist, 68% were treated by the nurses utilizing the behavioral modification techniques of desensitization, flooding, modeling, and operant methods. All patients were assessed before and after treatment. Treatment averaged ten sessions over a nine-week period, and the results indicated that the nurses treated the patients as successfully as psychiatrists. This example illustrated the overall conclusion in paraprofessional research: given good supervision and structured tasks, paraprofessionals can intervene effectively with mental-health patients.

USES OF PARAPROFESSIONALS WITH THE ELDERLY

It has only been in the last 15 years that paraprofessionals have been utilized in psychological and psychosocial interventions with

TABLE 5.1. Summary of Reviews on Paraprofessionals

Effectiveness:

   a. Paraprofessionals as effective as psychotherapists, academic counselors, and behavioral modifiers.
   b. Effectiveness is enhanced in structured tasks.
   c. Empathy and warmth are valued characteristics.
   d. Supervision enhances paraprofessional performance.

Populations Served:

   a. In and outpatient mental health
   b. Child and adolescent educational programs

Methodological Problems:

   a. Lack of control groups
   b. Lack of control for experimenter bias

elderly patients (Becker and Zarit, 1978; David and Ehrenpreis, 1981; Gatz, Hileman, and Amaral, 1984; Lichtenberg, Heck, and Turner, 1988; Santos et al., 1984; and Smyer, Cohn, and Brannon, 1988). In this section, the early usage of paraprofessionals in gerontological care will be reviewed and critiqued. This will be followed by an in-depth review of five demonstration programs in long-term care and by an in-depth presentation of a paraprofessional program.

Becker and Zarit (1978) trained older adults to be outpatient peer counselors. Their rationale focused on the fact that the similarities in age between the paraprofessional and client group might enhance the treatment intervention. The volunteers were 11 older adults who underwent ten 1 1/2-hour sessions focusing on developing empathy, warmth, and genuineness; they also received information about aging. Six older adults not undergoing the training served as the control group. Prior to the training, both groups were similar in levels of response on all measures. Following the intervention, the experimental group showed significantly increased levels of empathy and warmth, whereas the control group did not. Gatz, Hileman, and Amaral (1984) also advocated the usage of older adults as paraprofessional workers for elders living in the community. Their vision included a greater role than just individual counseling; they believed older paraprofessionals should become involved in community organization, gerontological advocacy, and casework. Additionally, the authors believed the paraprofessional role served as preventive mental health for the workers themselves, since it provided meaningful roles for them. Of all the studies they reviewed, however, only one was involved in long-term care. Nevertheless, both of these papers highlight the benefits of paraprofessionals working with community elderly–benefits that affect both the patient and the worker.

Santos et al. (1984) described their paraprofessional program, Coordinated Agency Resources for Elderly Services (CARES), that serves community elderly. This program, largely staffed by college student volunteers, provided a wide variety of services to the elderly (e.g., transportation, paperwork, referrals, and counseling). Paraprofessionals underwent four to six months of coursework on a variety of problems experienced by the elderly, and then they worked as a supervised intern. The authors highlighted the following aspects as unique: (1) a high priority on supervision, (2) actively seeking referrals from formal and informal services, and (3) extensive training of volunteers. In two years, CARES assisted 475 clients.

The work of the authors cited above caused others to attempt to define the possible usage of paraprofessionals in geriatric long-term care (David and Ehrenpreis, 1981; Brannon and Bodnar, 1988). David and Ehrenpreis stated that despite using paraprofessionals to provide mental-health services to the elderly, little attempt had been made to define the tasks appropriate for them. The authors divided paraprofessional characteristics into essential skills and a list of competencies. Active listening, the ability to recognize physical signs and symptoms indicating the need for medical attention, and making appropriate referrals were seen as essential skills. Competencies included a commitment to the elderly, knowledge of "normal" and "abnormal" aging, assessment abilities, ability to counsel and work with groups, understanding families, and knowing aging resources.

Brannon and Bodnar (1988) targeted long-term care in delineating potential roles for paraprofessionals. They listed seven possible areas of functioning: (1) working with families to inform them about long-term care; (2) helping with recreation needs; (3) helping patients communicate with long-term-care professionals; (4) encouraging basic health; (5) delivering counseling and/or behavior management; (6) helping to assess mental-health problems; and (7) helping with discharge planning. The authors suggested creating a new role in long-term care, the mental-health assistant.

INNOVATIVE EFFORTS IN LONG-TERM CARE

In Table 5.2, five innovative paraprofessional demonstration projects are highlighted. These programs will be reviewed and critiqued here. Paraprofessionals were recruited in a variety of ways. Bayer, Bresloff, and Curley (1986) and Moss and Pfohl (1988) utilized existing staff in new paraprofessional roles, while Mallya and Fitz (1987) introduced new paraprofessional staff into long-term care in their efforts to improve psychosocial care. Crose et al.

TABLE 5.2. Paraprofessional Demonstration Projects in Long-Term Care

<u>Authors</u>	<u>Program</u>
Bayer, Breshoff and Curley (1986)	Nursing assistants delivering psychosocial not physical care
Crose et al. (1987)	Older volunteers counseling mentally impaired
Mallya and Fitz (1987)	Individualized plans developed by paraprofessionals to improve functional status
Moss and Pfohl (1988)	Staff as visitors to long-term-care patients
Nagel, Cimbolic, and Newlin (1988)	Adolescent and older adults as counselors to depressed patients

(1987) and Nagel, Cimbolic, and Newlin (1988) utilized community volunteers in their programs.

Crose et al. (1987) introduced Project OASIS (Older Adults Sharing Important Skills), an attempt to help alleviate the shortage of mental-health services in long-term care by using trained volunteers. Volunteers were recruited through two seminars open to the public. From the 105 people who attended the seminars, 13 decided to participate in the program. An intensive pre-service training experience was utilized, and volunteers spent a six-hour day each week, for four weeks, learning about aging and mental-health problems. Lecture, experiential exercises, and modeling demonstrations were presented to teach counseling skills. Following the intensive training, supervision of counseling skills was continued by the project coordinators. Volunteers began intervening with patients at the level of friendly visitors. As they gained experience, they began to offer peer counseling services. The evaluation of the paraprofessionals' effectiveness was focused on 25 patients who had received direct one-to-one help from a volunteer over a period of time. In general, excess disability was reduced and increased functional abilities were displayed. Three problems were encountered, however. These included volunteer problems, a lack of long-term-care staff support, and funding problems. Volunteers were often frustrated by a lack of noticeable progress in patients, and when long-term-care staff was not intimately involved in the project, volunteer efforts were not successful.

Nagel, Cimbolic, and Newlin (1988) presented a methodologically sound intervention study in paraprofessional counseling with depressed long-term-care patients. A total of 20 volunteer counselors (ten elderly and ten adolescent) were trained in empathic listening, while another 20 volunteers (ten elderly and ten adolescent) were only given information regarding the aging process. Training for both groups consisted of six-hour sessions on consecutive weekend days. The 60 depressed long-term-care patients were selected if their Zung depression scale score was in the range of moderate depression (the patients were screened to eliminate those with neurologic deficits or overt psychosis). The 60 patients were placed in one of two treatment conditions (i.e., those receiving counseling from volunteers trained in empathic listening, and those receiving counseling from volunteers trained only in the aging process) or in a no-treatment control group. Counseling was given to long-term-care patients during two one-hour sessions each week, for five weeks. The major finding indicated that patients seen by the volunteers (those trained in empathy and those trained only in aging) improved on depression scores from pretest to posttest. Both elderly and adolescent counselors were found comparable in helping skills and therapeutic outcomes.

Mallya and Fitz (1987) described their three years of experience with Project Adapt, a mental-health service in long-term care that was funded by the Missouri Department of Mental Health. Paraprofessional therapeutic assistants were assigned to a long-term-care facility to deliver services to ten clients each, spending a minimum of 16 hours per week in the long-term-care facility. Paraprofessionals underwent an intensive two-week pre-service training program, followed by weekly training and monthly in-services. Project Adapt personnel identified 44 frequently occurring areas for patient improvement, ranging from eating to communicating with family. Within the long-term-care treatment team, individualized plans were developed. The major intervention focus by paraprofessionals was in the application of behavioral management plans. Project Adapt staff also created a Family Outreach Program designed to provide information and understanding to the family.

Four facilities participated in Project Adapt's evaluation, with three receiving programming and one serving as a control group. Five of the 36 control patients were rated as improved in their functioning (14%), whereas, in the treatment group, 93 of 120 were rated as improved (78%). One example of patient improvement included weaning the patient from having a catheter, so that he would utilize planned toilet times that increased toileting independence. Project Adapt also provided support to facility staff through monthly training programs attended by nursing assistants, licensed practical nurses, and registered nurses.

Twenty staff members–who were not giving direct care to long-term-care patients but were working in the organization–developed a Friendly Visitor Program at the Philadelphia Geriatric Center to improve psychosocial functioning in long-term-care patients (Moss and Pfohl, 1988). Regular monthly meetings for the 20 staff visitors were held to offer mutual support, to orient new visitors, and to discuss psychosocial concerns raised during visitations (e.g., death and dying, relationship problems). The visitors' aim was to develop friendships and not formal counseling relationships. A year after the program began, a questionnaire was distributed to the visitors. The visiting staff reported a number of satisfactions with the program, mostly in the meaningfulness of the relationship with the patient. The patients were quite satisfied as well, and developed close, confidant relationships with the visitors.

Bayer, Bresloff, and Curley (1986) described their grant funded "Enhancement Project," a one-year staff development program designed to improve the quality of psychosocial care to long-term-care patients. One out of every ten days, a nurse's aide came to work in a gold-colored lab coat that indicated that she was an enhancement aide for the day. During that day, the aide performed no physical care; instead, she provided only psychosocial care. This included eating and socializing with the patients, letter writing, helping transport patients to activities, and participating with them in recreational therapy programs. The enhancement aides also attended team conferences and meetings with families. Enhancement aides were assigned journal articles discussing psychosocial issues, and they were asked to keep a daily journal. At a six-month evaluation, the authors were delighted with the program. New, innovative care was being delivered, and patient response was enthusiastic. The program was funded again due to its success.

In this section, a variety of innovative uses of paraprofessionals were presented. In some cases, formal mental-health services were delivered (Crose et al., 1987; Mallya and Fitz, 1987; Nagel, Cimbolic, and Newlin, 1988). In other cases, informal support was offered (Bayer, Bresloff, and Curley, 1986; Moss and Pfohl, 1988). All of the programs described have obvious benefits, but there are also shortcomings with each. Two of the three formal programs targeted counselling as the only intervention offered. As Mallya and Fitz (1987) observed, however, there are a wide variety of psychosocial and functional needs in long-term-care patients and, to meet these needs, paraprofessional roles must be flexible and broad. Furthermore, it is necessary for paraprofessionals to be well integrated into the treatment team, or gains made in counseling are likely to have little carry-over. The more informal programs offer an excellent supplement to active psychosocial programs, but they are in no way substitutions for a comprehensive psychosocial approach. Still, the studies in using paraprofessionals in gerontology (and the innovative paraprofessional programs described) laid the foundation for the creation of a new use of paraprofessionals, as the mental-health workers in long-term care.

THE SHENANDOAH GERIATRIC TREATMENT CENTER PROGRAM

In the program described below, paraprofessionals worked in conjunction with professionals or under professional supervision (Christensen, Miller, and Munoz, 1978). Thus, a strong identification with psychological services was fostered. As in other programs, paraprofessionals were a major component in applying intervention programs, and a high priority was placed on supervision (Santos et al., 1984). Indeed, training, supervision, and evaluation were viewed as three highly interrelated activities. Supervision in this model was developmental. Skills and expertise increased as paraprofessionals received ongoing consultation and education. In this section, the selection process for a mental-health worker will be presented, along with the major stages in developing competent mental-health workers, the recommended areas of training, and the structure of supervision. Case reports will illustrate the paraprofessionals' work.

Mental-health workers were chosen from the nursing-assistant pool at the Shenandoah Center. Tellis-Nyak (1988) and Tellis-Nyak and Tellis-Nyak (1989) provided tremendous insight into the strengths and weaknesses of nursing assistants. Nursing assistants often share many of the SES (socio economic status) characteristics of the long-term-care patients, and it has long been thought that this is highly advantageous. Tellis-Nyak and Tellis-Nyak (1989) presented a typology of nursing assistants. One group of assistants they labeled as "Disaffected Endurers," and the other group as "Determined Strivers." It is from the Determined Strivers group that excellent candidates for a mental-health worker position can be found. Strivers, like endurers, often face tremendous personal hardships (e.g., poverty, poor educational background), but they separate themselves from endurers by their determination to succeed. In their work as assistants, they not only work hard but cultivate close, caring relationships with their patients. They are often eager for more knowledge about their patients as well as for promotional opportunities. The authors speculated that it is the determined strivers who make up a high percentage of the long-term-care staff exodus. When they cannot move up in the long-term-care facility, they move on. The mental-health worker role would allow long-term-care facilities to keep more of these employees by offering a more advanced position.

In Tables 5.3 and 5.4, the major areas of training given to mental-health workers at the Shenandoah Geriatric Treatment Center–and the major roles they fill–are listed. As shown in Table 5.3, training includes counseling, mental illness, dementia, caregiver experiences, common use of psychiatric drugs, behavioral modification, neuropsychology, grief, and conceptualizing cases. This translates into the following roles (see Table 5.4): counseling, behavior management, family and community outreach, administering neuro-

TABLE 5.3. Areas of Training for Mental-Health Workers in Long-Term Care

Counseling
  a. Empathy
  b. Warmth
  c. Genuineness
  d. Active listening

Major Mental Illness
  a. Schizophrenia/Delusional disorder
  b. Bipolar Disorder
  c. Major Depression

Alzheimers and other Dementias
  a. Cognitive effects
  b. Behavioral problems
  c. Caregiver burden and depression

Psychopharmacology
  a. Common antipsychotic medications
  b. Common antidepressant medications
  c. Common antianxiety medications

Behavioral Modification
  a. Positive reinforcement/Punishment
  b. Differential Reinforcement of Other Behavior (DRO)
  c. Time Out
  d. Shaping
  e. Chaining

Neurospychology
  a. Basic organization of cortex
  b. Use of tests
  c. Procedures and practice for standardized adminstration

Grief
  a. Phases: Shock, searching, sufffering, healing
  b. Stages: Denial, anger, bargaining, depression, acceptance

Case Conferences
  a. Organizing case material
  b. Presenting case material

TABLE 5.4. Major Roles of Mental-Health Workers in Long-Term Care

Individual Counseling

Behavior Management

Family and Commmunity Outreach

Administering Neuropsychological tests

Charting/Graphing effect of treatment plan

Group Counseling

Crisis Intervention

Supplemental shopping for patients

Helping with special activities

Aid patient communication with professional staff

psychological tests, crisis intervention, helping with activities, and aiding patient communication with professional staff. These roles and tasks were introduced slowly, in three stages, over a period of years. The major focus of training and basic training content will be briefly described below and supplemented by case examples.

The first step in introducing the mental-health worker program was to define it as an active, patient-centered, direct-service program. Mental-health workers were given two primary missions: (1) improve patients' quality of life and (2) actively treat problems. The dual role was important because it helped to balance the patients' needs and the staffs' needs. Two major tools were taught to the mental-health workers in order to better achieve their goals: basic counseling techniques and basic behavioral modification methods.

Quality of life was improved by providing a receptive, nurturing relationship with the patient. Counseling techniques helped to accomplish this. The mental-health workers were taught the value of listening. Initially, they were often eager to solve their patients' problems. In their early attempts to do exactly that, however, they often gave their patients messages that the problems were no longer appropriate to discuss. Through individual supervision sessions, didactic group sessions, and general discussions, the rationale for using counseling techniques were clarified.

The approach to counseling used here, as with many of the paraprofessional programs cited earlier, stems from the work by Carl Rogers (1957). Rogers highlighted the importance of the relationship between counselor and counselee. In order for that relationship to prosper, the counselor must display unconditional positive regard, empathy, genuineness, and be perceived in a trusting way by the counselee. Characteristics of this model, particularly empathy and listening skills, have been found to be significantly related to counselee improvement (Barrett-Lennard, 1981; Patterson, 1984). Charkhuff (1969, 1972) provided a comprehensive model for counseling skills training. Through that training, mental-health workers were able to change their orientation from expert and adviser to collaborative explorer of the counselee's issues and feelings. This counseling skill attainment can be accomplished only through lecture, observation, readings, and supervised practice. The following case illustrates how active listening gained the trust of this long-term-care patient and enabled an important counseling relationship to develop, thereby fostering a positive adjustment to long-term care by the patient.

Mrs. C.

Mrs. C., a 76-year-old, single, retired custodial worker entered long-term care when her sisters noticed that she was no longer cooking for herself, taking care of her personal hygiene, or heeding their advice to take better care of herself. In addition, Mrs. C. became somewhat suspicious of her sisters. Mrs. C. had a few chronic illnesses, and was ambulatory, but there was doubt about her cognitive abilities. On a neuropsychological assessment, it was revealed that Mrs. C. completed only four years of school and that her intellectual skills were in the low-average-to-borderline range. She was a poor learner, yet she retained the information she learned. At the time, her symptoms were more consistent with a major depression than with a progressive dementia.

In the long-term-care facility, Mrs. C. was subdued and withdrawn. The mental-health worker began visiting with her, engaging her in conversations and providing praise. Mrs. C. confided to the mental-health worker her feelings of loneliness at being separated from her home and her sisters. Additionally, she was afraid of certain staff members and patients. The mental-health worker encouraged Mrs. C. to discuss her feelings about having to leave home. Mrs. C. admitted her angry feelings toward her sisters and her guilt at being angry. She also spoke at length of her fears that she would end up a helpless patient and be mistreated by staff. Mrs. C. was provided considerable reassurance that caring staff were there to help. The mental-health worker began inviting Mrs. C. to therapeutic activities such as exercise, music, crafts, and a field trip. Mrs. C. began to attend to her self-care needs, and although she needed reminding and prompting, Mrs. C. complied with requests to dress and wash up. She resumed interest in handling small amounts of spending money and asked the mental-health worker to help her understand what she could and could not afford. The mental-health worker met weekly with Mrs. C. They kept a quantitative account of Mrs. C.'s involvement with activities and of her moods. Her adjustment to long-term care proceeded smoothly.

Behavior Modification

Behavior modification was taught to mental-health workers as a set of techniques whereby negative patient behaviors were reduced and positive behaviors were increased. Thus, when staff complained about particular patient problems that interfered with the patient's care and quality of life (resistiveness, hitting, verbal abuse), mental-health workers were taught to help plan and implement behavior modification treatment. The terminology used in behavior modification was not easily learned. In addition, it was necessary to explain the pace of treatment. That is, immediate solutions and changes are not provided. Mental-health workers were taught that improvements came only after consistent application of treatment. Initially, they were easily frustrated and lost confidence in the behavior plans. They needed frequent and considerable encouragement to stick with it. Later, when they could see the positive results, they were able to explain the process of treatment to the other staff. A brief overview of content taught to the mental-health workers is provided below.

As mentioned in the introductory chapter, behavioral modification has been widely used in long-term care (Hussian and Davis, 1985), and this section will serve only as a brief overview of what mental-health workers need to know. When analyzing staff behavior in most long-term-care settings, it is apparent that staff overuse punishment strategies and also reinforce undesirable behaviors. Reinforcement refers to the consequences of a behavior that lead to future increases in that behavior. Punishment, in behavioral modification terms, refers to the consequences of a behavior that lead to a future reduction in that behavior. Time-out procedures are an example of a punishment strategy. Two other useful concepts when applying behavioral modification in long-term care are shaping and chaining. Shaping refers to the rewarding of behaviors that are successive approximations of the desired behavior. In one of our programs, for example, a food reward was first given to an inactive man for simply walking five feet. Soon, he had to walk another five feet to get the reward; in a few months, he was walking a considerable distance to obtain the same small reward. Chaining refers to breaking a task into its component parts. An excellent example of this is Block et al.'s description (1987) of breaking dressing into 33 distinct behaviors. Providing reinforcement, such as praise, for each step increased dressing activity.

Behavior modification, like any intervention, must be aimed at the level of the patients. It can be useful to pitch behavioral plans to different levels of patients. In our program, we developed different typologies for three patient groups: (1) the moderately to severely demented; (2) the mildly cognitively disturbed group with psychiatric problems; and (3) the cognitively intact, personally troubled group. For the progressive dementia group suffering moderate-to-severe cognitive dysfunction, stimulus control was the most useful technique (Hussian, 1983). For the mildly cognitively disturbed group of patients who had behavioral disturbances, a mixture of reinforcement and punishment strategies worked best. The final group, the cognitively intact, mainly displayed problems with interpersonal relationships. This group's behavioral plans focused on using strategies to enhance cooperation among patients and on having the staff use an assertiveness approach during their verbal interactions with these patients. Mental-health workers are key personnel in getting a behavioral program started; collecting the quantitative data on the effectiveness of the program; and modeling the use of the behavioral techniques. The following case studies highlight the usage of behavior modification within each typology.

Type 1: The Moderately/Severely Demented Patient

Alzheimer's disease is one that produces enormous fear in its victims. This fear often leads to suspiciousness, catastrophic reactions (i.e., panic reactions), physical violence, and verbal hostility. Thus, reassurance and redirection may be the best intervention strategies. A good initial strategy is to help the patient feel safe and then get them involved in a new activity. Two aspects of the intervention should be considered to make it the most effective. First, noting any predictors or situations that commonly precede behavioral outbursts in the patient and, second, determining how best to change the environment.

Mr. S.

Mr. S. was a 73-year-old single man who had displayed progressive cognitive deterioration for two years, and then abruptly stopped eating and became severely impaired cognitively. He was then brought into long-term care. He was extremely anxious, pacing constantly, moving furniture throughout the building and trying to pull down the side rails in the hallway. Attempts were made to treat these symptoms with medications. While on Haloperidol, he developed Parkinsonian side effects, and, later, a trial of Lorazepam left him unsteady. Medications were discontinued, and a behavioral plan was introduced. It was hypothesized that Mr. S. needed considerable physical activity. Thus, a structured schedule was introduced that included a regular morning walk and participation in activity groups. In addition, a subset of chairs was put in an empty closet; when Mr. S. began to push furniture, he was asked to transport this small group of chairs to the dayroom. He was satisfied to complete this task and then allowed himself to be redirected to a new activity.

Type 2: Mild Cognitive Impairment; Behaviorally Disturbed

This group of patients has the cognitive abilities to remember unit routines and treatment plans and, thus, can be aware of potential rewards and punishers. A behavioral plan such as shaping, chaining, or differential reinforcement is often successful with this group.

Mr. G.

Mr. G., a 78-year-old single male, was admitted to our long-term-care facility after a long psychiatric hospitalization due to schizophrenia. During his early twenties, Mr. G. was committed to a state psychiatric hospital for wandering and disorganized thinking. He was kept in his room for a month; at the end of that time, he was catatonic. He was tube-fed and became extremely seclusive, with unintelligible speech and apparent hallucinations. With the advent of antipsychotic medications, he was finally treated with medication. He improved to the point where he was eating, drinking, and socializing, but he still remained somewhat seclusive. At our facility, he was noted to be oriented and able to follow commands. He wished, however, to spend his entire day lying in bed. The mental-health worker utilized a shaping technique to increase Mr. G.'s physical activity. Over the course of six months, Mr. G.'s walking improved from ten feet to one mile. Access to his bed for a rest was contingent upon his meeting the specified walking distance for that day. Thus, Mr. G. significantly increased his physical activity.

Type 3: The Cognitively Intact, Interpersonally Troubled Patients

This group of patients has good cognitive functioning, but severely troubled interpersonal relationships. They often have long histories of conflict-ridden relationships. Due to their need for significant physical assistance, they enter long-term care after they have alienated all potential caregivers in the community. Mrs. J. and Mrs. T. were two such women, and roommates as well. Both of them wanted to decide what channel the main lobby television was turned to, what the nurses schedule should be, and who should get the biggest plate at dinner. One insisted on playing the radio upon rising at 5:30 a.m., while the other would keep the lights on at night until 1:00 a.m. Daily, they complained bitterly about one another, and yet they had not had any success with other roommates.

A behavioral approach that rewarded cooperation was utilized. The plan stated that if staff either witnessed an argument between the two or heard complaints from either patient about the other, the two women would lose television-watching privileges for one day and be asked to remain indoors for that day. Within two weeks, the patients ceased hostilities toward one another and reached some compromises.

Setting limits and utilizing an assertiveness approach is an effective way for nursing assistants, practical nurses, and mental-health workers to deal with patients who are frequently verbally hostile. Mrs. O., a 69-year-old homemaker with severe arthritis and a seizure disorder, belittled the staff constantly. While they tried to accommodate her many demands, a good number of her requests were inappropriate. A behavioral contract was written outlining what responsibilities the staff had and what Mrs. O.'s responsibilities were. When Mrs. O. became verbally hostile, the staff was instructed to respond, "Mrs. O., I cannot work with you when you are verbally hostile. I will return in ten minutes to try to work with you again." As a result of the plan, Mrs. O.'s hostilities diminished greatly, and she began to meet more of her own needs.

The second major stage in developing mental-health workers was in teaching specific geriatric knowledge. Mental illness, dementia, and grief were focused upon. This stage was begun only after the mental-health workers were clearly comfortable with the use of basic counseling methods and behavioral techniques. The goal of this stage was to help mental health-workers understand specific problems and their varying treatments. The more advanced training also helped the mental-health workers to better understand why previously learned treatment techniques are effective. This was the easiest stage for the mental-health workers, because they were eager to learn. Material was once again presented in didactics, in individual supervision, and through modeling by the psychologist. A brief description of key knowledge is provided below.

Gold (1984) lamented that schizophrenia in the elderly was present, but all too often unaccounted for, in community care. Gold pointed out that a low, but persistent, risk of schizophrenia continues into old age. Furthermore, many schizophrenic patients who have suffered from the illness for decades end up in long-term-care facilities. Thus, schizophrenia in long-term care is commonplace. Nevertheless, in two recent books on mental health in long-term care, schizophrenia was barely discussed (Brink, 1990; Smyer, Brannon, and Cohn, 1988).

Not only do mental-health workers need training in counseling, but they also need education on symptoms and treatment of major mental illnesses, such as schizophrenia and manic-depressive illness. Schizophrenia's hallmark positive symptoms include hallucinations (almost always auditory, such as hearing voices that are not there) and delusions (fixed beliefs), which are often either grandiose or paranoid. The major negative symptoms include social withdrawal, blunted affect, and distant interpersonal relationships. This composite of symptoms does not meet the criteria for schizophrenia if they are due to seizures, stroke, head injuries, or any other known organic cause. Schizophrenia is not usually curable, but, even in the elderly, it is treatable. A paranoid delusional disorder, characterized by a firmly held belief that others are out to do them harm (but which is not accompanied by hallucinations, social withdrawal, or flat affect), is different from schizophrenia. It is not treatable with medications. Bipolar disease, known also as manic-depressive illness, has as its chief symptoms fluctuations between mania (i.e., grandiosity, flight of ideas, extreme energy) and depression. During either phase of the illness, but particularly during the manic phase, grandiosity, delusions, and hallucinations can be found. It is vital that this disease be differentiated from schizophrenia, since its drug treatment is one that is altogether different from the treatment for schizophrenia. In all cases, however, the mental-health worker can have a substantial impact. The important task is to slowly build a trusting and honest relationship over time.

Schizophrenic patients often need only a single, close confidant. The following case illustrates how the mental-health worker can effectively work with mentally ill elderly.

Mrs B.

Mrs. B. set herself on fire at the age of 55 because she heard God's voice tell her to do so. She was placed in a state psychiatric hospital for the first time in her life, and although her hallucinations were diminished by psychotropic medications, they were not eradicated. Ten years later, she was in a geriatric long-term-care facility. Her psychiatric symptoms were mostly negative symptoms of schizophrenia (i.e., blunted affect, withdrawal, decreased energy), but, on occasion, she would feel compelled to follow the voices' commands. These voices would typically tell her to stop eating or that she would soon die.

Prior to the onset of her schizophrenia, Mrs. B. was a high school graduate who had worked for years as a bookkeeper. She never married, and was devoted to her father. He died one year before she began to hear voices. She had one sister she had been close to; but now, Mrs. B. believed that her sister was also deceased.

The first task of the mental-health worker was to build a trusting relationship. Mrs. B. was a bright woman who enjoyed conversation. As the relationship developed, Mrs. B. told the mental-health worker what the voices were telling her. These included commands not to eat, to get a razor to cut herself, and to kill herself. Although Mrs. B.'s beliefs remained fixed, the mental-health worker could persuade Mrs. B. to eat and to take part in some recreational activities. The relationship provided enough safety that Mrs. B. confided that she would never kill herself while living at the facility; in fact, she stopped requesting a razor. Later, when Mrs. B. began to show symptoms of major depression (crying, apathy, declining concentration), the mental-health worker was able to notify the consulting psychiatrist, and a successful trial of an anti-depressant was carried out. The mental-health worker thus offered Mrs. B. safety and a secure relationship that offered support in times of distress.

Medication Treatment

Since a major form of treatment for schizophrenia, bipolar disease, and major depression is medication, mental-health workers must become familiar with these therapies and their side effects. All medication has side effects, and the medicines used to treat these diseases are no exception. Indeed, the side effects are dangerous if left unchecked or unrecognized. Antipsychotic medications (Chlorpromazine, Thioridazine, Thiothixene, Haloperidol, and Fluphenazine) are used to treat schizophrenia and are also used during the extreme phases of manic depression. Major side effects include rigidity, restlessness, and, if used long-term, tardive dyskinesia (an involuntary movement disorder). Chlorpromazine and Thioridazine can be especially sedating and predispose the patient to hypotensive episodes, or cause falls or strokes (Kock-Weser et al., 1983a). Lithium is the drug prescribed most often for manic depression. A major risk of lithium is receiving too much of it and suffering from toxic symptoms. These include tremors, nausea, abdominal pain, slurred speech, and confusion (Koch-Weser et al. 1983a). Toxicity can be produced by such changes as sodium restriction, decreased water intake, or diuretic treatment.

Antidepressant medications (Amitryptaline, Doxepin, Imipramine, Nortyptyline, Desipramine, Maprotiline, Amoxapine, Trazodone, Fluoxetene) can also have worrisome side effects. Hypotension, cardiac problems, and anticholinergic symptoms (visual problems, sweating, gastric upset) are the most common side effects. The different antidepressants have different risks associated with them (Koch-Weser et al., 1983b).

Anti-anxiety medications (Flurazepam, Temezapam, Oxazepam, Diazepam, and Lorazepam) may be the most overused psychoactive drugs in long-term care. They are beneficial only for short-term relief of anxiety (Koch-Weser et al., 1983b), not for long-term use. Indeed, they are known to produce excessive sedation, diminished energy, and loss of sexual desire when used over long periods. Anti-anxiety medications may also worsen depression and dementia.

Dementia

Since dementia is pervasive in long-term-care patients, mental-health workers need to understand the diagnostic process and symptom progression in their demented patients. Since Alzheimer's is the most common form of dementia, it was taught in some depth to the paraprofessionals. Alzheimer's is a progressive illness causing severe neuropsychological and behavioral symptoms, leading to death. The cause of the illness remains unknown, and its final diagnosis rests only upon brain biopsies. The course of the illness varies considerably between individuals, but a general description follows. The onset of the disease is slow and subtle, with cognitive and personality changes as early symptoms. Typically, episodes of confusion and memory loss are among the earliest symptoms, as are outbursts of anger, suspiciousness, or withdrawal. As the disease progresses, it produces a number of severe symptoms. The major cognitive symptoms include: (1) aphasia, which refers to a language disturbance where both the production of meaningful language and the comprehension of language are reduced; (2) apraxia, which refers to the inability to carry out planned motor movements, such as taking a bath or opening a box; and (3) agnosia, which refers to a disturbance in the recognition of objects and people.

Behavioral problems are also extremely common in Alzheimer's patients. These include increasing dependency and, with it, heightened suspiciousness. Wandering, night waking, hiding things, violent emotional outbursts, and physical attacks on caregivers are all common, as are incontinence and decreased self-care (Lichtenberg and Barth, 1989). Alzheimer patients are often very fearful (Gwyther, 1985). They cannot understand what is happening to them, nor can they comprehend their environment. As a result, reassurance and redirection are the most useful interventions. (Once again, active listening skills are very useful for the mental-health worker.) The following is an example of using redirection and reassurance.

Mrs. I.

Mrs. I., a 75-year-old widowed, retired factory worker suffering from Alzheimer's disease, was pacing frantically one afternoon. The activities therapist wanted to take Mrs. I. to crafts, but Mrs. I. was headed for the front door. The mental-health worker interceded and asked Mrs. I. what was wrong. "Oh," Mrs. I. exclaimed, "I have to get home to get the wood stove going so my babies don't freeze." "Yes, I understand," said the mental-health worker, "because I have a wood stove, too. But, you know, it has been awfully warm these last few nights, and I have not had to use mine. Plus, see how light it is? It is way too early to be going home. Why don't we go to crafts group?" Mrs. I. did go to her crafts group, and did not mention the wood stove anymore that day. The first task of the mental-health worker was to provide security through reassurance and then to utilize the memory disorder so as to redirect Mrs. I. to her crafts group.

Grief

Mental-health workers were taught about grief to help them identify healthy versus unhealthy grieving, and to increase their ability
to counsel grieving patients. Grief will be described here. In a later
chapter, on psychotherapy, case examples will be provided. Grief is
the psychological process involved in reacting to loss. Long-term-
care patients are often grieving any number of losses, including the
following:

* Loss of spouse
* Loss of adult child
* Loss of health
* Loss of independent living
* Loss of friends
* Loss of economic freedom
* Loss of a pain-free existence
* Loss of occupation/hobbies
* Loss of own life due to terminal illness

Grief is all too often a poorly understood phenomenon, but understanding the grief process is critical when involved in giving psychological or psychosocial care to the elderly. Stages of grief (Kubler-Ross, 1969; Simos, 1979) and phases of grief (Tatelbaum, 1984)
are two useful, mutually compatible ways of understanding the
phenomenon. The stages of grief outlined by Kubler-Ross and Simos include denial, shock, anger, bargaining, depression, and acceptance. There is not an orderly transition through these stages;
instead, an individual will bounce back and forth between them.
    Phases of grief are more orderly, and they include shock, search-
ing, suffering, and healing. Shock is a protective, numbing experience of disbelief that occurs early after a loss and generally lasts for
two to three weeks. Searching refers to the mechanism of "looking
for" the deceased. This is done through vivid dreams, obsessively
reviewing the time spent with the deceased, and actually looking for
the deceased. Suffering refers to the deep anguish felt after the
reality of the loss becomes fully experienced; it typically occurs
eight to twelve weeks following a loss. Healing from grief means

the person is living fully again in the present. In each phase of grief, the stages described by Kubler-Ross and Simos are evident.

Several other points, however, must also be realized about grief. First, a new loss–or threat of loss–revives the pain of grief from previous losses. It is not uncommon, then, for an elderly person who is grieving the loss of independence to discover themselves missing a deceased parent or friend. Second, grief takes much longer than people expect. Normal grief can last two to five years. Third, a major depression is not part of normal grieving; rather, it is grief plus major depression. Signs to look for in elderly grievers with major depression include self-criticism, low self-esteem, and excessive pessimism. Fourth, in order to work with grieving patients, mental-health workers must be comfortable with tears and with anger.

The third stage of mental-health worker development increased their level of independence and responsibility. This was accomplished by training them to be involved in neuropsychological test administration and in efforts aimed at family and community outreach. Test administration and family outreach required mental-health workers to be confident of their ability to communicate and to be disciplined in their approach. Therefore, their responsibilities were expanded only after all other areas were mastered. These last roles, when learned well, became integral parts of long-term-care treatment.

Family and Community Outreach

It has long been known that families do not simply abandon their elderly loved ones (Shanas, 1979). However, when a loved one enters a long-term-care facility, family members often withdraw and lose their involvement with the patient. When the mental-health workers reach out to the family, providing them with an empathic ear, they also enable the patient to have continued family contact. The following two cases are dramatic illustrations of the importance of mental-health workers serving as liaisons between patients and families.

Mrs. L.

Mrs. L., a 72-year-old widowed homemaker, entered our long-term-care facility after falling and breaking her hip and shoulder, followed by a bout of pneumonia that left her unable to return home. She suffered from many physical problems, including anemia, chronic pain from osteoporosis and rheumatoid arthritis, hypertension, and renal insufficiency. Upon entering the facility, Mrs. L. was verbally hostile and refused to help with her own physical-care needs. She requested pain medications around the clock. A neuropsychological assessment found her to have significant cognitive strengths and weaknesses. Verbal reasoning and recall memory were in the intact range, whereas she was unable to perform complex visuospatial tasks. Emotionally, she was lonely and feeling hopeless, but did not suffer from a major depression.

The mental-health worker began visiting Mrs. L., who was an extremely family-oriented woman. She lost both of her parents during adolescence, and was very close to her siblings. Of the five original siblings, only two were living, and they were 70 miles away. She had not spoken to them in a year, due to her decline in health. Mrs. L. had one daughter who lived across the country. The mental-health worker concentrated on two major goals with Mrs. L. First, she helped Mrs. L. to focus on her family in a productive way, and, second, she drew up a behavioral plan to increase Mrs. L.'s involvement in her own personal care. She spent a considerable amount of time allowing Mrs. L. to discuss and reminisce about her family. The mental-health worker helped Mrs. L. write to her family, phoned family members, and arranged for calls to Mrs. L. Later, the mental-health worker took Mrs. L. for a day-long visit at her sibling's home. When Mrs. L.'s daughter came to town, the mental-health worker spent time updating her on her mother's condition.

When the mental-health worker began to work with Mrs. L., the staff was overwhelmingly convinced that Mrs. L.'s family had abandoned her and wanted nothing to do with her. This was, quite simply, inaccurate. The family had stopped contacting Mrs. L. because she had become belligerent over the telephone. They were extremely interested in her care, and in maintaining a relationship with her.

A functional assessment was conducted by Mrs. L.'s physician and nurses to determine which self-care tasks she could perform. Indeed, she was physically capable of transferring from her wheelchair to a sitting chair and to the commode, and she could feed and dress herself quite capably. These became her responsibilities, and although she complained of pain, she began to perform these tasks regularly.

Mrs. M.

Mrs. M. was a 71-year-old widowed retired secretary who suffered from a late-adult-onset bipolar disorder in her sixties, and was placed in our long-term care when her son, who was caring for her, became overburdened. He felt utterly overwhelmed, placed her in long-term care, and four weeks later moved 600 miles away without saying goodbye. Prior to her admission, she was often found wandering on the highway and was noted to have experienced several bouts of severe depression. A neuropsychological assessment performed immediately after admission found that, while she had good verbal reasoning and memory skills, her visuospatial abilities and topographical orientation were severely impaired. Thus, it was likely that she would get lost if she began wandering. A social service note documented the son's inability to maintain contact and stated that she had no family support.

Mrs. M. was pleasant and very cooperative with the staff. She spent much of her time reading and participating in the recreational group activities offered. She was not eating or sleeping well, however. She was often ruminating about her son's decision to place her in long-term care. The mental-health worker took her out of the building for lunch, and to look at Mrs. M.'s old neighborhoods, but her visuospatial deficits made it difficult for Mrs. M. to recognize the places. Mrs. M. became increasingly agitated, becoming short-tempered with the more confused patients in the facility. One day, she received a package of clothes from her son, along with a note from him that said he was moving away. Mrs. M. began to display heightened hostility. She also began to hallucinate and was placed on Haloperidol. Her increased aggressiveness continued. Haloperidol was stopped and an anti-depressant and lithium were started. Her hostility lessened, and normal grief surfaced.

She began to confide in the mental-health worker about her feelings of abandonment. After talking extensively with Mrs. M., the mental-health worker learned that Mrs. M. did still have family in the area. Mrs. M.'s mother and brother were living, and although none of the three had been close throughout their adulthood, the mental-health worker contacted both of Mrs. M.'s relatives. Both relatives were delighted to hear from her. The mother was 93 and, although in a long-term-care facility, was cognitively intact. A visit was arranged, and the mental-health worker took Mrs. M. to see her mother. They had a warm and positive visit and decided to visit every six to eight weeks. They celebrated birthdays and holidays. In our long-term-care facility, Mrs. M. returned to taking part in recreational activities and, through practice, learned a short walking route outside, which she was able to enjoy without supervision. She became close to the staff, and her depression resolved.

Long-term-care patients must continue to venture out into the community as long as they are able. No one benefits from being inside of one place all of the time, and, indeed, renewed enthusiasm can come to patients who enjoy a lunch out or a shopping trip in town. Mental-health workers can also play a significant role in bringing community volunteers in for regular visits and programming. This is a critical component to enhanced psychosocial care (Tellis-Nyak, 1988).

Neuropsychology

In Chapters 2 and 3, the use of neuropsychology was described in detail. The mental-health worker can fill the valuable role of administering various tests, particularly screening measures. Practice, live supervision by the psychologist to check the accuracy of the mental-health worker's use of standardized test administration, and ongoing supervision to ensure that new questions or needs are addressed promptly are all essential.

Rather than casting the mental-health worker's testing role as the result of understaffing, it is important to value the benefits of the role. The patient may in fact be more receptive to being tested by a team member who is seen daily and who performs many roles on the unit. The mental-health worker can bring about the patient's future cooperation with all types of tests and procedures by making this early testing experience a positive one. Often, if the patient perceives that the mental-health worker has time, he or she will engage in extended discussion of concerns that might go unnoticed by other team members until much later. Adjustment to long-term care is, therefore, facilitated by the mental health-workers' sensitivity to confidentiality issues and by their role as a liaison between the patient and the team.

Concluding Remarks

As can be seen from Tables 5.3 and 5.4, there are quite a number of roles and responsibilities that a mental-health worker can fill in long-term care. Clearly, however, ongoing training and supervision are required.

In Table 5.5 are some of the components necessary for supervising mental-health workers. Again, it is fruitful to think of the developmental approach to supervision described by Christensen, Miller, and Munoz (1978). Pre-service training does not, and cannot, ever fully prepare a paraprofessional. Rather, to start with, a mental-health worker should be given circumscribed duties and focused training, such as in counseling and behavior management. Supervision, both individual and group (when more than one mental-health worker is employed), must be didactic; new areas must be taught as

TABLE 5.5. Necessary Components of Supervision of Paraprofessionals

Weekly and ongoing

Review 5 chart notes

Paraprofessionals observe in-vivo modeling by professional

Supervisor directly observes paraprofessionals

Supplement with readings and didactics

Supervisor must provide emotional support to reduce burnout

the mental-health worker adapts to the initial tasks. One of the best ways for mental-health workers to learn is to directly observe the psychologist in practice (e.g., counseling, implementing plans, and providing feedback to patients, staff, and family). Individual cases and the case presentation method can be a powerful illustrator of textbook facts. Mental-health workers should also read primary source material.

Medical record charting, detailed in narrative progress notes on the frequency of goal behaviors, is a skill that must be taught to mental-health workers. Professional consultants need to read the medical record to get an understanding of the patients' problems. What is typically found, however, are notes filled with useless jargon. This includes statements such as "the patient is disoriented" or "the patient is uncooperative." What the professional needs, and what mental-health workers learn to provide, are behavioral descriptions of interactions with patients rather than generalized conclusions. The following structure of a progress note is offered: (1) Describe the nature of the contact with the patient; (2) Describe the patient's affect; (3) Describe the patient's behavior; (4) Describe the intervention used and the patient outcome. Five notes per week is a reasonable goal and notes should be read by the supervisor.

The second crucial aspect of charting and record keeping involves collecting quantitative data on the patient in order to assess the effectiveness of a treatment plan. Too often plans are implemented and then we simply ask "Is this working?" In long-term care this is bound to lead to distortions and effectiveness is not adequately addressed. In contrast, mental-health workers can be trained to oversee the use of graphs and frequency counts to evaluate treatment objectively and quantitatively.

Finally, it is important that supervisors provide mental-health workers with emotional support. The mental-health worker role distinguishes itself from the Nursing Assistant role, thus, mental-health workers are often left without the peer support nursing assistants give to one another. Supervisors must provide active listening to the frustrations, fears, and self doubts of the mental-health workers.

The number of patients per mental-health worker should vary depending on the level of the patient. This role is most useful in helping the physically ill, cognitively intact group, and the mild, moderate, and severe cognitively impaired group that retain ambulatory skills.

SUMMARY

In this chapter, a new paraprofessional role in long-term care was introduced. The mental-health worker role is a promising one for improving psychological functioning in long-term-care patients. An overview was provided of the roles mental-health workers can fill and in the areas of training needed. Case examples illustrated the usefulness of this role. Finally, a supervisory structure was described.

REFERENCES

Balch, P., and Solomon, R. (1976). The Training of Paraprofessionals as Behavior Modifiers: A Review. *American Journal of Community Psychology, 4,* 167-178.

Barrett-Lennard, G.T. (1981). The Empathy Cycle: Refinement of a Nuclear Concept. *Journal of Counseling Psychology, 28,* 91-100.

Bayer, M., Bresloff, L., and Curley, D. (1986). The Enhancement Project: A Program to Improve the Quality of Residents' Lives. *Geriatric Nursing, July/August,* 192-195.

Becker, F., and Zarit, S.H. (1978). Training Older Adults as Peer Counselors. *Educational Gerontology, 3,* 241-250.

Block, C., Boczkowski, J.A., Hansen, N., and Vanderbeck, M. (1987). Nursing Home Consultation: Difficult Residents and Frustrated Staff. *The Gerontologist 27,* 443-446.

Brannon, D., and Bodnar, J. (1988). The Primary Caregivers: Aides and LPNs. In M. Smyer, M. Cohn, and D. Brannon (Eds.) *Mental Health Consultation in Nursing Homes.* NYU Press: New York, 192-212.

Brink, T. (1990) (Ed.) *Mental Health in the Nursing Home,* The Haworth Press: Binghamton, NY.

Brown, W.F. (1974). Effectiveness of Paraprofessionals: The Evidence. *Personnel and Guidance Journal, 53,* 257-263.

Christensen, A., Miller, W.R., and Munoz, R.F. (1978). Paraprofessionals, Partners, Peers, Paraphernalia, and Print: Expanding Mental Health Service Delivery. *Professional Psychology, May,* 249-270.

Crose, R., Duffy, M., Warren, J., and Franklin, B. (1987). Project OASIS: Volunteer Mental Health Paraprofessionals Serving Nursing Home Residents. *The Gerontologist, 27,* 359-362.

David, D.D., and Ehrenpreis, T.G. (1981). Mental Health Paraprofessionals in Gerontology. *Journal of Gerontological Social Work, 3,* 3-12.

Durlak, J.A. (1979). Comparative Effectiveness of Paraprofessional and Professional Helpers. *Psychological Bulletin, 86,* 80-92.

Gatz, M., Hileman, C., and Amaral, P. (1984). Older Adult Paraprofessionals: Working with and in Behalf of Older Adults. *Journal of Community Psychology, 12,* 347-358.

Gold, D. (1984). Late Age of Onset Schizophrenia: Present but Unaccounted for. *Comprehensive Psychiatry, 25,* 225-237.

Gwyther, L. P. (1985). *Care of Alzheimer's Patients.* American Health Care Association: Washington, DC.

Hussian, R. A. (1983). Stimulus Control in the Modification of Problematic Behavior in Elderly Institutionalized Patients. *International Journal of Behavioral Geriatrics, 1,* 33-42.

Hussian, R. A., and Davis, R. (1985). *Responsive Care: Behavioral Interventions with Elderly Persons.* Research Press: Illinois.

Karlsruher, A.E. (1974). The Nonprofessional as a Psychotherapeutic Agent: A Review of the Empirical Evidence Pertaining to His Effectiveness. *American Journal of Community Psychology, 2,* 61-77.

Kock-Weser, J., Thompson, T., Moran, M., and Nies, A. (1983a). Psychotropic Drug Use in the Elderly (part 1). *New England Journal of Medicine,* 134-138.

Kock-Weser, J., Thompson, T., Moran, M., and Nies, A. (1983b). Psychotropic Drug Use in the Elderly (part 2). *New England Journal of Medicine,* 134-138.

Kubler-Ross, E. (1969). *On Death and Dying.* Macmillan Co.: New York.

Lichtenberg, P.A., and Barth, J.T. (1989). Depression in Elderly Caregivers. *Medical Psychotherapy, 3,* 147-156.

Lichtenberg, P.A., Heck, G.C., and Turner, A.B. (1988). Medical Psychotherapy With Elderly Psychiatric Inpatients: Uses of Paraprofessionals in Treatment. *Medical Psychotherapy, 1,* 87-93.

Mallya, A., and Fitz, D. (1987). A Psychogeriatric Rehabilitation Program in Long-Term Care Facilities. *The Gerontologist, 27,* 747-751.

Marks, I.M., Connolly, J., and Hallam, R.S. (1973). Psychiatric Nurse as Therapist. *British Medical Journal, 3,* 156-160.

Moffic, H.S., Patterson, G.K., Laval, R., and Adams, G.L. (1984). Paraprofessionals and Psychiatric Teams: An Updated Review. *Hospital and Community Psychiatry, 35,* 61-67.

Moss, M.S., and Pfohl, D.C. (1988). New Friendships: Staff as Visitors of Nursing Home Residents. *The Gerontologist, 28,* 263-265.

Nagel, J., Cimbolic P., and Newlin, M. (1988). Efficacy of Elderly and Adolescent Volunteer Counselors in a Nursing Home Setting. *Journal of Counseling Psychology, 35,* 81-86.

Patterson, C.H. (1984). Empathy, Warmth, and Genuineness in Psychotherapy: A Review of Reviews. *Psychotherapy, 21,* 431-438.

Rogers, C.R. (1957). The Necessary and Sufficient Conditions of Therapeutic Personality Change. *Journal of Counseling Psychology, 21,* 95-103.

Santos, J.F., Hubbard, R.W., McIntosh, J.L., and Eisner, H.R. (1984). Community Mental Health and the Elderly: Service and Training Approaches. *Journal of Community Psychology, 12,* 359-368.

Shanas, E. (1979). Social Myth as Hypothesis: The Case of Family Relations of Old People. *The Gerontologist, 19,* 3-9.

Simos, B. (1979) *A Time to Grieve.* Family Service Association of America: New York.

Smyer, M., Cohn, M., and Brannon, D. (1988). *Mental Health Consultation in Nursing Homes.* NYU Press: New York.

Tatelbaum, J. (1984). *The Courage to Grieve*. Harper Collins.

Tellis-Nyak, V. (1988). *Nursing Home Exemplars of Quality: The Paths to Excellence in Quality Nursing Homes*. Charles Thomas: Springfield, IL.

Tellis-Nayk, V., and Tellis-Nayk, M. (1989). Quality of Care and the Burden of Two Cultures: When the World of the Nurse's Aide Enters the World of the Nursing Home. *The Gerontologist, 29*, 307-313.

Chapter 6

Alcohol Abuse

Alcohol abuse is a significantly more frequent problem among medically ill and long-term-care elderly than it is among healthy community-dwelling elderly (Brody, 1982; Curtis et al., 1989; Janik and Dunham, 1983; Maddox, 1988; Myers et al., 1982; Schuckit, 1977; Ticehurst, 1990; Zimberg, 1984). It has only been in the last 15 years, however, that alcoholism in elders became widely recognized by addictions professionals. In one prominent alcohol journal, there was only one article on the topic between 1940 and 1959; there were 13 articles between 1960 and 1969. Articles on alcohol abuse in the elderly only became common in the 1970s (Maddox, 1988). Maddox (1988) summarized the National Institutes of Mental Health's (NIMH) study that utilized four sites and a sample of 8,000 community dwelling elderly. Prevalence rates for alcoholism ranged from 0.9%-4.6% in men over age sixty to 0.1%-0.7% of women. Twenty-five percent of men and four percent of women claimed to have alcohol abuse problems at some time during their life. This was based upon interview data; alcohol abuse and dependence criteria were taken from the *Diagnostic and Statistical Manual* (DSM III). Myers et al. (1982) studied 928 non-institutionalized older adults. Fifty-three percent of the sample were abstainers, and 1% claimed to have an active drinking problem. An additional 5% said they had suffered from previous alcohol abuse problems. An open-ended, face-to-face interview method was used to determine the presence of alcohol abuse. Given that both studies relied on self-report methods, these prevalence rates could be underestimates of the problem. Ticehurst (1990) noted that survey results indicate that non-drinking increases from 22% in the 30s to 80% in those over 80, thereby leading health practitioners to believe that elderly

111

do not abuse alcohol. However, Schuckit's early work (1977) suggested that between 2% and 10% of the elderly population are alcoholics and that 9% of all alcohol abusers in treatment were elderly.

Alcoholism is a serious health problem in the nation's elderly. Alcoholism is the third-leading killer of adults in the United States (Benshoff and Roberto, 1988), and is the third most common psychiatric diagnosis in elderly men (Ticehurst, 1990). Schuckit and Pastor (1978) found that elderly alcohol abusers typically present to medical/surgical units with problems. In a survey of 113 consecutive Veterans' Administration (VA) admissions, 20% of men met the criteria for alcoholism, with 9% actively drinking. Brody (1982) estimated that 10%-15% of elderly seeking attention in a medical office abuse alcohol. Curtis et al. (1989) surveyed 417 consecutive admissions to the Johns Hopkins Hospital, using standardized screening instruments. Overall, 21% of those over the age 60 were abusing alcohol. The authors also investigated physician detection of the alcohol abuse. Forty-five percent of non-elderly were correctly identified by physicians, whereas only 27% of elderly alcohol abusers were correctly identified. Gender effects were evident, in that no elderly women were diagnosed as alcoholic by the house officer. The authors concluded that routine screening instruments are needed. Similarly, Schuckit et al. (1980) found that physicians failed to detect 90% of elderly alcoholics in their sample.

Alcoholism may have its highest prevalence in long-term-care facilities. Curtis et al. (1989) found that alcoholism ranged from 30%-47% in gero-psychiatric in-patients. Studies of nursing homes have estimated alcoholism rates at between 15% and 60% (Brody, 1982; Maddox, 1988), but there are no systematic studies of alcohol abuse prevalence in long-term care. Due to their focus on obvious physical problems, long-term-care staff are not likely to recognize symptoms of alcoholism. As a result, they underestimate alcohol-related problems.

The few longitudinal studies performed have given encouragement that alcoholism can be treated in the elderly; these studies have also raised a typology of "early" versus "late" onset alcoholics. Nordstrom and Berglund (1987) tracked 55 male alcoholics for 20 years after their first admission to the hospital. At followup, 42%

still abused alcohol, 38% were social drinkers, and 20% were abstainers. In a three-year followup, only 20% of active alcoholics seen at a medical unit became abstainers. Once again, a self-report methodology was used. The reporting of such a high percentage of alcohol abusers as "social drinkers" runs against widely held beliefs that most alcohol abusers cannot control their intake. Whether the findings are reflective of true facts or of response bias, these authors have provided some of the only longitudinal data.

Studies on the prevalence of alcoholism in the elderly have revealed two types of alcoholics: early and late onset (Brody, 1982; Gomberg, 1990; Zimberg, 1984). Two-thirds of elderly alcoholics are represented in the early-onset group. These individuals have had longstanding alcoholic histories that continued into later life. The more severe long-term effects of alcohol (discussed in a later section) are more likely in this group. The late-onset alcoholics developed their drinking problem in late life. Authors have hypothesized various stressors associated with late-onset alcoholism, and these include depression, bereavement, retirement, loneliness, physical illness, and pain. However, both groups are believed to be able to respond to the same type of treatment.

DEFINING ALCOHOLISM

Alcoholism in the elderly is often hidden due to its subtle presentation. Nevertheless, Beresford et al. (1988) described four aspects of the addiction to alcohol.

The first aspect, *tolerance*, refers to the alcoholic's need to increase drinking by 50% in order to achieve the same effect. For example, a man who had four drinks a day may find himself, over time, drinking a pint or two. Typically, the alcoholic is seeking a feeling of escape and drinks until this feeling is acquired.

The second aspect, *withdrawal*, refers to physical symptoms that follow six to twelve hours after the blood alcohol level has decreased. Common symptoms include increased blood pressure, low-grade fever, sweating, tremors, nausea, and increased anxiety. Beresford et al. (1988) are quick to point out that other medications, particularly anti-anxiety medicines (see Chapter 4) and other sedatives, mask the withdrawal syndrome. They also caution that total withdrawal from alcohol can be very dangerous and needs to be monitored closely by medical personnel.

The third aspect, *loss of control* over the drinking behavior and the preoccupation with guilt and shame, is the most subtle aspect of the diagnosis. Often, this loss of control leads to severe loneliness and isolation. This phenomenon can be observed in alcoholics that begin an evening determined to have one drink, and end up becoming drunk.

Finally, *social decline*, and the loss, or at least the severe straining, of familial and other close relationships is the last aspect of this definition. Therefore, it is important to carefully assess the patient's psycho-social history, both prior to and after the onset of the alcoholism.

Maletta (1982) grouped drinking problems into several categories when defining alcoholism. These overlap significantly with the definition by Beresford and his colleagues. The five categories are: (1) symptoms that developed as a result of drinking (e.g., blackouts, tremors); (2) psychological dependence and health problems related to alcohol use; (3) problems with relatives, colleagues, friends, or neighbors that are related to alcohol use; (4) problems with employment or finances; and (5) problems with law enforcement officials. Problem drinking is described as applying to people who exhibit behaviors from more than one of the listed categories.

MYTHS ABOUT ALCOHOL AND THE ELDERLY ALCOHOLIC

Many myths about alcohol abuse in the elderly are held by the lay public, health care, and long-term-care professionals. The most common myths will be cited here, and refuted. It is the ongoing propagation of many of these myths that keeps alcohol abuse in the elderly a hidden problem in all settings (community, hospital, and in long-term care).

Myth #1: Drinking Won't Hurt the Elderly

As can be seen in Table 6.1, alcohol has many toxic effects on its elderly abusers. Since alcohol affects so many parts of the body,

TABLE 6.1. Physical Problems Associated with Alcoholism in the Elderly

Benshoff and Roberto (1988)
1. Neurologic Ailments: Peripheral neuropathy, cerebellar degeneration, sleep disturbances, sexual dysfunction.
2. Gastrointestinal: Cirrhosis of the liver, pancreatitis (pain, nausea, vomiting), upper respiratory infections, stomach, colon problems.
3. Cardio-vascular: Alcohol exacerbates all heart problems.

Eckhardt and Martin (1986)
1. Brain Dysfunction: 50-70% alcoholics have cognitive impairment; 90% develop severe dementia.

Hubbard, Santos and Santos (1979)
1. 22% of alcohol abusers presented as functionally senile due to overdose.

Gomberg (1990)
1. Aging: Lower amounts of alcohol produce higher blood levels.
2. Decreases in liver and kidney functioning makes alcohol stay in the body longer.

Hartford and Samorajski (1982)
1. Sleep: Reduced REM sleep and reduced stages 3 & 4 sleep (deeper sleep)
2. Nervous System: Myopathy, susceptibility to infection, nutritional and vitamin deficiencies.
3. Brain Impairment: Basal ganglia, hippocampus.

discussing them is often viewed as an "organ recital." Thienhaus and Hartford (1984) described the physical changes that affect the distribution of alcohol in an older adult. At age 25, for example, 61% of the human body is composed of water, but by age 70, this percentage drops to 53%. Because alcohol is rapidly distributed through the body water compartment after ingestion, less alcohol is needed by an older adult to produce acute intoxication. One thing that makes alcohol abuse symptoms so subtle in the elderly is that they consume less alcohol than do younger alcoholics (Schuckit, 1977) In addition, decreases in liver and kidney functioning make alcohol remain in the body longer (Gomberg, 1990; Benshoff and

Roberto, 1988), underscoring the fact that alcohol, when abused, is a killer. In the elderly, alcohol kills from chronic debilitating and deteriorating conditions rather than from acute events. Thienhaus and Hartford (1984) concluded that the aging body is more susceptible to the toxic effects of alcohol. As can be seen in Table 6.1, alcoholism produces damage to the central nervous system, the gastrointestinal system, and the cardiovascular system. The most common problems are cirrhosis of the liver, pancreatitis, heart dysfunction, and neurologic damage.

Eckardt and Martin (1986) estimated that 50%-70% of elderly alcoholics have cognitive impairment and that 9% develop severe dementia. They cited visuospatial functioning and abstract reasoning as the most consistently impaired areas of cognitive functioning. Hubbard, Santos, and Santos (1979) stated that almost a quarter of elderly alcohol abusers presented to the hospital as functionally senile. When the patients were withdrawn from alcohol, their cognition was, in general, greatly improved. However, alcohol-related damage to such brain areas as the basal ganglia affect motor functioning and balance. Other severe side effects of alcoholism are its direct impact on sleep, sexual functioning, and functioning of the stomach and colon.

Myth # 2: Without the Alcohol, the Older Adult Would Be Lonely or Depressed

This myth is often stated as: "Why take away their only pleasure (i.e., drinking)?" The truth, of course, is that alcohol is a central nervous system depressant, and that, over time, it causes increased depression and loss of pleasure. Myers et al. (1982) reported that in their community sample of elderly alcohol abusers, 22% stated that their relationships with others suffered significantly. In addition, those with alcohol problems were significantly less satisfied with their life than those without drinking problems. Schuckit et al. (1980), in their three-year study of alcohol abuse and treatment, found the alcohol abusers to be more prone to depression than those without drinking problems. It is precisely because a major hallmark of alcohol abuse in the elderly is that it leaves them lonely and isolated, that most authors view socialization and grief work as necessary components to alcohol treatment (Brody, 1982; Kofoed et al., 1987; Sumberg, 1985; Zimberg, 1984). In long-term care, one group of alcoholic patients will come into the facility having no community or family support, saddled with severe debilitating chronic illness, and significant cognitive deficits. A second group will come in with significant physical health needs and a lack of community support, but few cognitive problems. This group, often suffering from depression, is more likely to have their alcoholism overlooked.

Myth # 3: Alcohol Treatment Does Not Work with the Elderly

This myth is often stated as: "Alcoholics are too set in their ways to change." Here, an overview of treatment effectiveness will be reviewed, and, in a later section, discussion of specific aspects of treatment will be explored. Research has repeatedly shown that older alcoholics respond just as well-if not better-to treatment than do younger adults (Atkinson and Kofoed, 1982; Benshoff and Roberto, 1988; Janik and Dunham, 1983; Schuckit, 1977; Zimbero, 1984). Janik and Dunham reported on the results from 550 alcoholism treatment programs, for a total sample of 3,163 older alcoholics (aged 60 and up) and 3,190 younger alcoholics. Self-report and counselor ratings were used to determine followup results 180 days after the completion of inpatient treatment. Men, overall, had a poorer treatment outcome than women, and older adults had a significantly better treatment outcome than did middle-aged ones.

Atkinson and Kofoed (1982) and Kofoed et al. (1987) have reported on a series of studies in which older alcoholics were more likely to complete treatment successfully and to maintain sobriety for longer periods. In his study of all alcohol treatment programs for the state of Washington, Schuckit (1977) found that while 73% of the elderly who started treatment completed it, only 40% of younger patients did so. Schuckit did not speculate as to the reason for this. In contrast to younger adults, however, elderly alcohol abusers may experience more directly the ill effects of the alcohol abuse (physical decline, cognitive dysfunction, and social decline). As a result, they may be more motivated or ready to enter treatment.

DETECTING ALCOHOLISM

Detecting alcoholism depends upon the clinician and long-term-care staff learning the subtle cluster of symptoms that are present in older alcoholics. In their early study, Rosin and Glatt (1971) investigated the consequences of alcohol excess in the elderly. Only one of the 36 patients suffered from delirium tremens, a common withdrawal symptom in younger adults; 66%, however, displayed self-neglect, 33% displayed falls; 31% had confusion; 11% were aggressive; and 56% had their family relationships terminated. Not all of the above problems, however, were due to alcohol abuse. Indeed, many of these problems are experienced by a considerable number of nonalcohol-abusing elderly. Nevertheless, observing a constellation of these problems may help to detect alcohol abuse. In Table 6.2, the common nonspecific presentations of alcohol abuse in the elderly are noted (Atkinson and Kofoed, 1982; Hartford and Samorajski, 1982; Ticehurst, 1990; and Wattis, 1981).

As can be seen in the table, behaviors are separated into three categories: general health, interpersonal changes, and alcohol-related behaviors. The list of health problems common in the elderly alcoholic is a lengthy one. The more obvious problems, and ones that should raise the clinician's suspicions, include poor grooming, unexplained falls, bruises or burns, and malnutrition. Other common problems in this group that can be obtained through laboratory examination are heart and liver disease, seizures, chronic obstructive pulmonary disease, accidental hypothermia, and peptic ulcer disease (Atkinson and Kofoed, 1982; Ticehurst, 1990). Alcohol

TABLE 6.2. Nonspecific Presentations of Alcohol Abuse in the Elderly

General Health: Poor grooming, incontinence, myopathy, falling, accidental hypothermia, seizures, malnutrition, diarrhea, unexplained bruises or burns, pepticulceration, heart and liver disease, chronic obstructive pulmonary disease.

Interpersonal: Confusion, aggression, termination of family relationships.

Alcohol: Preoccupation with drinking, rapid intake, alcohol used as medicine, using alcohol alone, protecting alcohol supply.

abuse is one of several conditions to rule out when a patient presents with symptoms of dementia. Wattis (1981) reported on seven cases of alcoholism that were initially undetected. In one case, an 81-year-old woman was admitted to the hospital by her daughter, who stated that her mother suffered memory problems and frequent falling. The daughter later found out that her mother drank heavy quantities of wine and scotch each day. Hartford and Samorajski (1982) found that 28% of dementia patients had undiagnosed alcoholism. Safety-risk behaviors are obviously of great concern to the long-term-care industry. Accidentally setting fires, a common occurrence among elder alcoholics, are tragic when they occur in long-term care.

Interpersonal changes are another area for clinicians to assess in the elderly. As mentioned earlier, social decline is part of alcoholism. This is often displayed by aggression and hostility toward family members, especially when the topic of alcohol is addressed. Rosin and Glatt (1971), in their early study, found that 56% of elderly alcoholics had at least one family relationship terminated by their drinking. Intermittent and unexplained periods of confusion are also classic signs of alcohol abuse.

The alcoholic's relationship with the alcohol is another area of diagnostic importance (see Table 6.2). Alcohol sometimes replaces other people in the role of comforter and supporter, and, thus, alcoholics protect their alcohol supply. The alcoholic often hides the alcohol problem as part of the denial. Alcohol is sometimes used as medicine, to decrease pain and discomfort. Alcoholics are preoccupied with their drinking. This preoccupation causes them to use alcohol alone, and to rapidly ingest the alcohol.

Use of Screening Measures to Detect Alcoholism

Curtis et al. (1989), in their diagnostic study, concluded that the routine use of screening instruments is needed in order to more accurately detect alcoholism in the elderly. Two screening measures will be discussed here (See Tables 6.3 and 6.4).

The CAGE Questionnaire (see Table 6.3), described by its author (Ewing, 1984), was developed in 1970 and is a most efficient and effective screening device. The questionnaire is made up of four simple questions about attitudes and behaviors related to the indi-

TABLE 6.3. Alcohol Screening Measure (CAGE Questionnaire)

C–Have you ever felt you ought to Cut down on your drinking?   (Y)

A–Have people Annoyed you by criticizing your drinking?   (Y)

G–Have you ever felt bad or Guilty about your drinking?   (Y)

E–Have you ever had a drink first thing in the morning to steady
your nerves or get rid of a hangover (Eye-opener)?   (Y)

CAGE SCORE > or = 2: suspicion of alcoholism

vidual's drinking. A score of two affirmative responses raises the suspicion of alcoholism, whereas a score of three of four affirmative responses is almost always a sure sign of alcoholism. The original data gathered on the CAGE consisted of comparing responses of 16 alcoholic with 114 non-alcoholic randomly selected medical patients. A second study of 166 male alcoholics revealed the CAGE to be a valid screening instrument with a sensitivity of 85% and a specificity of 100%. Bush et al. (1987) studied 518 patients admitted to the orthopedic and medical services of a community-based hospital during a six-month period. The criterion measure used for alcohol abuse was the standard criteria from the DSM III. The CAGE, and three laboratory tests, were compared for their ability to detect alcohol abuse. The laboratory tests were very insensitive, whereas the CAGE questionnaire was highly valid. The CAGE had a sensitivity of 85% and a specificity of 89%. Curtis et al. (1989) found the CAGE to be highly useful in detecting elderly alcohol abusers.

The Michigan Alcohol Screening Test (MAST), a 25-item instrument, was developed to provide a consistent and quantifiable method to detect alcoholism (Hedlund and Vieweg, 1984; Selzer, 1971). All questions are presented in a yes-no format. Porkorney, Miller, and Kaplan (1972) selected ten out of the 25 questions and developed the Brief Michigan Alcohol Screening Test (BMAST) (see Table 6.4). Internal consistency for the BMAST was reported at 0.80 and 0.60 on samples of all-age alcoholics. Willenbring et al. (1987) conducted an investigation of the MAST and its various short forms in a study aimed at screening for alcoholism in the

TABLE 6.4. Alcohol Screening Measure (Brief Michigan Alcohol Screening Test)

1. Do you feel you are a normal drinker? (N)

2. Do friends and relatives think you are a normal drinker? (N)

3. Have you ever attended Alcoholics Anonymous (AA)? (Y)

4. Have you ever lost friends or girlfriends/boyfriends because of drinking? (Y)

5. Have you ever gotten into trouble at work because of drinking? (Y)

6. Have you ever neglected your obligations, your family or your work for two or more days in a row because you were drinking? (Y)

7. Have you ever had Delerium Tremens (DT's), severe shaking, heard voices or seen things that weren't there after heavy drinking? (Y)

8. Have you ever gone to anyone for help about your drinking? (Y)

9. Have you ever been in a hsopital because of drinking? (Y)

10. Have you ever been arrested for drunk driving after drinking? (Y)

BMAST > 4: suspicion of alcoholism

elderly. They compared 52 consecutive older adults (age ≥ 60) admitted to aVeterans' Administration alcohol-treatment program with 33 controls (non-alcoholics) admitted for medical reasons. The BMAST was the best of all short MAST forms in detecting alcoholism in the sample. When using a cutoff score of four, the BMAST had a sensitivity rate of 91% and a specificity rate of 83%. Age and education were not significantly correlated with BMAST scores.

Detecting Alcoholism: Use of the Gatekeeper Method

"Gatekeepers," a term used in community social service programs to describe people who are in a position to identify high-risk elders (e.g., non-traditional referral sources), is a model that can be applied directly to long-term care. Raschko (1990) presented a decade of his community program in Spokane, Washington, that makes use of meter readers, bank personnel, fuel dealers, and others in identifying troubled elderly. Nineteen percent of the referrals were for alcohol abuse. The program works because alcoholics, due to denial, will not refer themselves for services. Gatekeepers are trained in spotting problems common in the elderly and their symptom presentation. Upon encountering a situation that raises their suspicion, the gatekeeper contacts the clinician and makes a referral. Community elderly, of course, preserve their right not to accept treatment, but often they are very willing to allow professionals to aid them. Sumberg (1985) also underscored the importance of widening the network of people who can identify the problems. In long-term care, this applies directly to groups of workers such as custodians, who are not traditionally thought of as part of the treatment team. Because of alcohol abusers' secretiveness, drinking problems *do* go undetected in long-term care. However, the contents of one's garbage (such as empty bottles of liquor) and the direct observations of the custodial staff are rich sources of information. By utilizing the custodial staff as gatekeepers, more of the alcohol problems in the elderly will be discovered. This will be illustrated again later in a case study.

INTERVENTION AND TREATMENT ISSUES

Families often unwittingly act in ways that aid the alcoholic in denying the problem and, thereby, help to perpetuate the alcohol abuse (Dupree, Broskowski, and Schonfeld, 1984; Hubbard, Santos, and Santos, 1979; Rathbone-McCuan and Triegaardt, 1979; and Wattis, 1981). The following are some common reactions by family members that actually encourage the drinking:

- Rescuing the alcohol abuser from the painful consequences of their drinking and not holding them responsible for their actions.
- Stigmatizing the alcohol abuse and making the drinker feel that the problem is shameful.
- Feeling hopeless, believing that elderly drinkers cannot be helped.
- Believing that drinking is one of the few pleasures left to the elderly person.

• Mistaking the diagnosis. Alcohol abuse that results in confusion in the drinker makes it appear as if the drinker has a primary degenerative condition, such as Alzheimer's disease.

Hubbard, Santos, and Santos (1979) found that the use of alcohol by older adults was encouraged by significant others because of medicinal myths and (i.e., the belief that it is "therapeutic" for alcohol intake to increase in the later years).

Rathbone-McCuan and Triegaardt (1979) found that adult children often felt too guilty if they did not give in to their parents' drinking demands. Wattis (1981) found that treatment for the older alcoholic was thwarted by adult children who were also abusing alcohol.

Marion and Stefanik-Campisi (1989) described the several pitfalls that inhibit professionals from making the proper diagnosis of alcoholism. Not surprisingly, many of the findings paralleled the ones mentioned above. It is no different in long-term-care facilities. Administrators, physicians, psychologists, social workers, nurses, nursing assistants, and the rest of the long-term-care staff also fall prey to these stereotypic myths about alcohol and the elderly.

Riddell's paper (1984) focused on methods to get the reluctant alcoholic to participate in treatment once the alcohol problem was identified. This is commonly referred to as the "intervention." Riddell's intervention consisted of three parts: individual confrontation, group intervention, and implementation of the plan (usually by admitting the alcoholic for acute treatment). The author cautioned that individual confrontation is only effective when the clinician has four tools: (1) A knowledge base of alcoholism; (2) facts regarding the individual's problems and symptoms; (3) understanding of the fear and panic experienced by the alcoholic when the suggestion is made to give up drinking; (4) leverage (i.e., something or someone important in the person's life to use as motivation or threat, such as losing one's spouse or car). Although the intervention should carry a positive and hopeful tone, the clinician must be specific and assertive in addressing the alcohol abuse and its effect on the abuser's life.

A group intervention should involve three to six people who have a meaningful relationship to the alcoholic. It is important for the group to be direct and honest. The individuals of the group can tell the alcoholic that they know that alcohol is interfering with his/her life and health (as well as that of the group) and that he/she needs treatment. A group intervention is often more likely to break the alcoholic's denial than is individual confrontation.

Marion and Stefanik-Campisi (1989) also focused on the intervention. They emphasized the importance of developing trust with the patient. Trust, they stated, is created by firm, direct, and honest patience. In order for trust to work over time, they stress the need for feedback, coupled with gentle persuasion. They also stressed the creation of a situation for the patient that intensifies the experience of the alcoholism. This can include the removal of support systems, such as the patient's family. Finally, these authors stress the need for the alcoholic to enter a treatment facility.

Rathbone-McCuan and Bland (1975) and Rathbone-McCuan and Triegaardt (1979) reported on their years of clinical experience in the treatment of elderly alcoholics. Three themes were evident in the treatment process. First, spouses must come into the treatment process. Second, polypharmacy, the use of a variety of drugs and medicines (as well as alcohol) must be evaluated and appropriately reduced. Finally, families that are estranged during earlier years can often be brought back into contact with the alcoholic now that treatment has begun.

Dupree, Broskowski, and Schonfeld (1984) described two unique and effective treatment efforts. Dupree and his colleagues focused on treating the late-onset alcoholic in their Gerontology Alcohol Project, a day treatment program. Over a two-year period, 406 referrals were made and 153 met the criteria for later-life-onset alcohol abuse. Only 48 (31%) agreed to treatment, with another one-half dropping out before completing treatment. Thus, 24 patients completed this unique program. Treatment was based on behavioral and self-management techniques. Four treatment modules were developed. The first analyzed the drinking behavior, identifying common antecedents to drinking and developing the behavior chain from general behavior to specific drinking behavior. Module 2 addressed self-management techniques in high-risk situations (e.g., cues, urges, relapse, depression, anger, and anxiety). Module 3 educated the patients on the medical, psychological, statistical, and theoretical aspects of alcohol abuse. The last module focused on general problem solving. Pre- and posttesting revealed the following results: (1) patients that completed the program learned the material from the different modules; (2) alcohol consumption was significantly reduced, both in the program and at followup; and (3) patients increased the size of their social network.

Kofoed et al. (1987) tested their hypothesis that elderly alcoholics would respond better to treatment in special elderly peer groups than in mixed-age groups and compared the outcomes of two groups of older alcoholics (24 in a mixed-age outpatient group and 25 in an elderly-only group). Each group received a 30-day inpatient program, followed by the outpatient group program. One year later, they compared the two groups. Sixty-eight percent of the patients in the elderly-only group remained in the treatment program, whereas only 17% of those in the mixed-age group did so. A blind retrospective review of records was performed. The treatment group had longer periods of sobriety than did the dropouts. When members of the treatment group did relapse, they were willing to get increased help and to once again begin abstaining from alcohol. In contrast, members of the dropout group did not get additional help. Though very promising results were produced, this sample was a small one, and generalizability is limited.

The following are two case illustrations of alcohol abuse in long-term care.

Mrs. S.

Mrs S., a 70-year-old three-time divorcee and retired store clerk, entered a long-term-care facility after spending two months in the hospital. Severe osteoporosis had made Mrs. S. wheelchair-dependent ten years earlier, and she had recently fallen and broken several bones after losing control of her wheelchair on a ramp. She underwent a bilateral hip replacement, yet, due to her physical limitations, she entered a long-term-care facility. Mrs. S.'s history was significant for family mental illness. Her father died when she was a young girl, while her mother suffered from many bouts of major affective disorders, spending the last ten years of her life in a psychiatric institution. Mrs. S. had married three times, and divorced each husband after a short time. She had no children.

In her young adulthood, Mrs. S. suffered from Hodgkins disease, but it went into remission. Severe osteoporosis began to cause her pain and fractures during her fifties. At the time of her admission to the Shenandoah Geriatric Treatment Center, she had many chronic medical problems. These included hiatal hernia, peptic ulcer disease, demoral addiction, bilateral hip replacement, and osteoporosis. She had fallen countless times, but apparently had never suffered a head injury.

Mrs. S. had a comprehensive neuropsychological assessment, revealing overall intellectual functioning in the average range, with no outstanding strengths or weaknesses. Visuospatial and verbal-recall memory scores were in the unimpaired range. The only areas of deficit were mild impairments on tasks of mental flexibility, such as in complex visuomotor tracking and in set changing. Mrs. S. reported no dysphoria and, thus, appeared to be having no significant emotional problems.

This patient appeared to make a smooth transition to long-term care during her first six months. She was engaging with the staff, and with her cognitive strengths, she was easy to converse with. She was tolerant of all of the other patients, would help direct the confused patients, and would socialize with the more intact patients. One persistent problem, however, was chronic pain that caused her to request narcotic pain medications. She had previously been addicted to Demerol, which eventually led to development of psychotic symptoms. Thus, she was given non-narcotic medications.

Mrs. S. began to spend considerable time outside the facility and off the long-term-care facility grounds. Concurrent with that development was a change in her behavior. She began to violate safety rules by smoking in her room and in her bed. She became extremely moody: sweet and delightful at times, and angry and nasty at others. She also displayed symptoms of grandiosity and hyperactivity.

In a search for a cause of these behavioral changes, no infections, diseases, or psychiatric conditions were found. Finally, the custodial workers were asked if they had noticed any of the changes. Indeed, they had. They brought to our attention the fact that Mrs. S.'s trash had been loaded with empty beer cans and whisky bottles for many weeks. The staff had missed the warning signs, such as gastrointestinal problems (hiatal hernia and peptic ulcer disease are common in alcohol abusers). Symptoms of alcohol abuse often mimic psychiatric symptoms.

Armed with this knowledge, the staff began to discuss the situation with Mrs. S. However, as might be expected, she was not receptive to this one discussion and left the facility. One week later, she set her hotel bed on fire, and was committed to a hospital for alcohol treatment.

Mrs. N.

Mrs. N. was a 68-year-old who was committed for treatment at a community hospital when she began saying, "I will blow my brains out." Her husband stated that he had seen her functional ability deteriorate over the preceding 12 months. He said there was a marked increase in her confusion, short-term memory loss, agitation, erratic behavior, and delusional and suicidal statements in the three weeks before commitment. She ruminated over the deaths of her family members, apparently unable to resolve her losses. Earlier, she had been a person who enjoyed outings, wanted to be "on the go," and enjoyed being with people. Recently, she had withdrawn from all social activities, and was possessive of her husband's time by requiring that he stay home with her, instead of agreeing to go out with him (as she had done during previous years).

After initial treatment at the community hospital, Mrs. N. remained delusional and paranoid. She believed that the hospital staff were out to harm her and that her deceased parents were still living. Although she denied being sad or depressed, she became tearful easily upon the mention of a recently deceased sister. She was resistant to the idea of remaining in the hospital for treatment, even though she was considered in need of long-term-care treatment. Her first marriage had been in her 30s, but 12 years later her husband died as a result of myocardial infarction. At the age of 53, she began a relationship with her current husband, by common-law marriage. Ten years prior to the admission, her brother had been killed in an altercation. One sister died a year prior to admission. Only four months prior to the admission, the sister she was closest to also died.

For at least three months prior to admission, she experienced severe back, hip, and leg pain that was attributed to a documented radiculopathy. She overmedicated herself by using alcohol, analgesic, and anxiolytic prescriptions obtained from multiple physicians-without her husband's knowledge.

Upon admission to the long-term-care facility, her treatment team determined that multiple factors contributed to her level of functional disability. First, she was still grieving the loss of her two sisters, and spoke as if the death of her brother (ten years ago) remained very painful to her as well. Second, her back, leg, and hip pain were exacerbated by her unresolved grief and depression and, in turn, also contributed to her heightened anxiety and to her fear that she would be admitted to surgery and die (at the same university hospital where her sister died). Third, her pain contributed to a pain-depression-pain cycle by causing her to avoid interesting activities and social interaction in order to remain in her bed. Finally, her overall level of cognitive functioning appeared to be premorbidly low due to lack of education; currently, this functioning was even lower, due to depression, overmedication with pain and anti-inflammatory drugs, alcohol abuse, and a possible underlying organic dementia.

Several factors made assessment and treatment of Mrs. N. difficult. Due to paranoid beliefs, she was uncooperative with many diagnostic procedures. Her low level of cognitive functioning, her memory impairment, and limited life experiences made it difficult for her to understand the jobs of the staff members or even to remember their names. Her cognitive deficits impaired her ability to resolve her grief, because she appeared to forget her grief until the therapist mentioned one of her deceased family members to her.

Five days after her admission, she was formally evaluated using a dementia screening battery. On the Geriatric Depression Scale, her responses reflected an attempt to appear "well," with repeated explanations that she was "ready to go home now." She denied her current depression by focusing on her activities prior to her illness, instead of admitting that her mood and her level of functioning had declined during the past year. On the Mattis Organic Mental Syndrome Screening Examination, her scores were in the "Defective" range on all subtests–with the exceptions of an intact score on naming objects and sentence repetition and of a mild impairment score on comprehension. Although her history of illiteracy made it difficult to interpret cognitive test results, she nevertheless had deficits in orientation and simple problem solving that suggested a decline from previous functioning. Her lack of insight regarding her condition was reflected by her inability to understand that her husband felt she needed treatment and by her persistent efforts to "bribe" the physician to discharge her, promising him a large sum of money.

In the facility, Mrs. N. became gradually more willing to get involved in activities. Yet she eventually opted to stay in her room due to both her leg pain and to her desire to avoid contact with the other patients, whom she considered to be "strangers." One month after her admission, 25 milligrams (q.h.s.) of Elavil was started for the treatment of her depression. By two months after admission, her activity level and interpersonal interactions had increased, she stopped asking for wheelchair assistance, and she eventually walked without her cane, on occasion.

With decreased pain, her activity level increased, and Mrs. N. finally agreed to receive supervision in her home and to stop using alcohol. This change was a major factor in enabling her to be placed back into her home with her husband just two-and-a-half months after admission.

A home assessment performed two weeks after Mrs. N. went home revealed that she was receiving help from a neighbor, as needed, while staying at home alone part of the day. Her mood was good, she was oriented regarding the way to get assistance from her neighbor, and she had reduced heavy housework to an appropriate level (given her back pain). Her husband administered prescribed medications to her, and all alcohol and excess medications were thrown away. Her husband, who thought she would not be able to live at home again, was very satisfied with her progress.

REFERENCES

Atkinson, R.M., and Kofoed, L.L. (1982). Alcohol and Drug Abuse in Old Age: A Clinical Perspective. *Substance and Alcohol Actions/Misuse, 3*, 353-368.

Benshoff, J.J., and Roberto, K.A. (1988). Alcoholism in the Elderly: Clinical Issues. *Clinical Gerontologist, 7*, 3-15.

Beresford, T.P., Blow, F.C., Brower, K.J., Adams, K.M., and Hall, R.C. (1988). Alcoholism and Aging in the General Hospital. *Psychosomatics, 29*, 61-72.

Brody, J.A. (1982). Aging and Alcohol Abuse. *Journal of the American Geriatrics Society, 30*, 123-126.

Bush, B., Shaw, S., Cleary, P., Delbanco, T.L., and Aronson, M.D. (1987). Screening for Alcohol Abuse Using the CAGE Questionnaire. *The American Journal of Medicine, 82*, 231-235.

Curtis, J.R., Geller, G., Stokes, E., Levine, D.M., and Moore, R.D (1989). Characteristics, Diagnosis, and Treatment of Alcoholism in Elderly Patients. *Journal of the American Geriatrics Society, 37*, 310-316.

Dupree, L.W., Broskowski, H., and Schonfield, L. (1984). The Gerontology Alcohol Project: A Behavioral Treatment Program for Elderly Alcohol Abusers. *The Gerontologist, 24*, 510-516.

Eckardt, M.J., and Martin, P.R. (1986). Clinical Assessment of Cognition in Alcoholism. *Alcoholism: Clinical and Experimental Research, 10*, 123-127.

Ewing, J.A. (1984). Detecting Alcoholism: The CAGE Questionnaire. *Journal of the American Medical Association, 252*, 1905-1907.

Gomberg, E.L. (1990). Drugs, Alcohol, and Aging. In *Research Advances in Alcohol and Drug Problems* (T. Kozlowski, Ed.). Vol. 10. Plenum Press.

Hartford, J.T., and Samorajski, T. (1982). Alcoholism in the Geriatric Population. *Journal of the American Geriatrics Society, 30*, 18-24.

Hedlund, J.L., and Vieweg, B.W. (1984). The Michigan Alcoholism Screening Test (MAST): A Comprehensive Review. *Journal of Operational Psychiatry, 15*, 55-64.

Hubbard, R.W., Santos, J.F., and Santos, M.A. (1979). Alcohol and Older Adults: Overt and Covert Influences. *Journal of Contemporary Social Work, March,* 166-170.

Janik, S.W., and Dunham, R.G. (1983). A Nationwide Examination of the Need for Specific Alcoholism Treatment Programs for the Elderly. *Journal of Studies on Alcohol, 44*, 307-317.

Kofoed, L.L., Tolson, R.L., Atkinson, R.M. Toth, R.L., and Turner, J.A. (1987). Treatment Compliance of Older Alcoholics: An Elder-Specific Approach is Superior to "Mainstreaming." *Journal of Studies on Alcohol, 48*, 47-51.

Maddox, G.L. (1988). Aging, Drinking and Alcohol Abuse. *Generations, Summer,* 14-16.

Maletta, G.J. (1982). Alcoholism and the Aged. In *Encyclopedia Handbook of Alcoholism* (W. Pattison and G. Kaufman, Eds.). Gardner Press: New York, 779-791.

Marion, T.R., and Stefanik-Campisi, C. (1989). The Elderly Alcoholic: Identification of Factors That Influence the Giving and Receiving of Help. *Perspectives in Psychiatric Care, 25*, 32-35.

Myers, A.R., Hingson, R., Mucatel, M., and Goldman, E. (1982). Social and Psychologic Correlates of Problem Drinking in Old Age. *Journal of the American Geriatrics Society, 30*, 452-456.

Nordstrom, G., and Berglund, M. (1987). Aging and Recovery from Alcoholism. *British Journal of Psychiatry, 15*, 382-388.

Porkorney, A., Miller, B., and Kaplan, H. (1972). The Brief MAST: A Shortened Version of the Michigan Alcoholism Screening Test. *American Journal of Psychiatry, 129*, 342-345.

Raschko, R. (1990). Gatekeepers Do the Casefinding in Spokane. Unpublished manuscript.

Rathbone-McCuan, E., and Bland, J. (1975). A Treatment Typology for The Elderly Alcohol Abuser. *Journal of the American Geriatrics Society, 23,* 553-557.

Rathbone-McCuan, E., and Triegaardt, J. (1979). The Older Alcoholic and the Family. *Alcohol Health and Research World, Summer,* 7-12.

Riddell, G.C. (1984). Interventions and Treatment of Elderly Alcoholics. *Generations, 24,* 30-37.

Rosin, A.J., and Glatt, M.M. (1971). Alcohol Excess in the Elderly. *Quarterly Journal of Studies on Alcoholism, 32,* 53-59.

Schuckit, M.A. (1977). Geriatric Alcoholism and Drug Abuse. *The Gerontologist, 17,* 168-174.

Schuckit, M.A., and Pastor, P.A. (1978). The Elderly as a Unique Population: Alcoholism. *Alcoholism: Clinical and Experimental Research, 2,* 31-38.

Schuckit, M.A., Atkinson, J.H., Miller, P.L., and Berman, J. (1980). A Three-Year Follow-up of Elderly Alcoholics. *Journal of Clinical Psychiatry, 41,* 412-416.

Selzer, M. (1971) The Michigan Alcoholism Screening Test: The Quest for a New Diagnostic Instrument. *American Journal of Psychiatry, 127,* 1653-1658.

Sumberg, D. (1985). Social Work with Elderly Alcoholics: Some Practical Considerations. *Gerontological Social Work Practice in the Community: Journal of Gerontological Social Work, 8,* 169-181.

Thienhaus, O.J., and Hartford, J.T. (1984). Alcoholism in the Elderly. *Psychiatric Medicine, 2,* 27-41.

Ticehurst, S. (1990). Alcohol and the Elderly. *Australian and New Zealand Journal of Psychiatry, 24,* 252-260.

Wattis, J.P. (1981). Alcohol Problems in the Elderly. *Journal of the American Geriatrics Society, 29,* 131-134.

Willenbring, M.L., Christensen, K.J., Spring, W.D., and Rasmussen, R.(1987). Alcoholism Screening in the Elderly. *Journal of the American Geriatrics Society, 35,* 864-869.

Zimberg, S. (1984). Diagnosis and Management of the Elderly Alcoholic. *Alcoholism and Drug Abuse in Old Age in Alcohol and Drug Abuse* (R. Atkinson, Ed.) American Psychiatric Press: Washington, D.C., 23-33.

Chapter 7

Sexuality in Long-Term Care

There are many widespread myths and misconceptions about sexuality in the elderly (George and Weiler, 1981; Kaas, 1978; Ludeman, 1981; Masters and Johnson, 1981; and Steinke and Bergen, 1984). This section will describe those myths and compare them with facts about sexuality and the elderly. Following this, research on sexuality and sexual expression in long-term care will be reviewed and critiqued. An innovative approach to assessing an elderly person's ability to participate in sexual relationships will be described and illustrated through case examples.

The biggest and most pervasive myth is that sexuality is not characteristic of older people and that older adults are asexual (George and Weiler, 1981; Kaas, 1978; Masters and Johnson, 1981). The second erroneous belief is that sexuality, when continued into later life, is wrong, sinful, or morally perverse. Finally, aging is often thought to lead to impotence or to other irreversible sexual problems.

In actuality, there are some physiological changes that affect sexuality in older adults, but, sexual capacity is lifelong. In Table 7.1, the most common physiological changes in older men and women are listed (Comfort, 1974; Fazio, 1988; Ludeman, 1981; Masters and Johnson, 1981). Schover (1985) provided an in-depth description of the components of sexuality and aging, and her work will be reviewed here. Three components that she described were sexual desire, sexual arousal, and orgasm. Sexual desire, she stated, remains relatively stable as one ages. Sexual arousal, however, becomes slower and less intense with aging. For older men, the ejaculation weakens during orgasm, and semen is expelled with less force. Martin (1981) proposed a similar, but more expanded, de-

TABLE 7.1. Normal Age-Related Physical Changes in Sexual Organs

Men	Women
• Arousal is slower and less intense	• Arousal is slower and less intense
• Takes longer to reach full penile engorgement	• Reduced size of cervix and uterus
• Decreased expulsive pressure	• Reduced volume of lubricating fluid
• Decreased volume of fluid expelled during ejaculation	• Thinning of vaginal walls
• Reduced ejaculatory demand	
• Lengthened refractory period	
• Long periods of celibacy will lead to some atrophy	

scription of the necessary criteria for sexual functioning to occur. First, the anatomical and physiological processes involved in the sexual response must be adequate. Second, the person must be exposed to stimuli having erotic significance. Third, the person must have erotic reactions to the stimuli. Fourth, there must be desire for sexual participation, followed by cooperation of an interested partner.

As can be seen in Table 7.1, men actually experience more aging changes than women do. Older men take longer to reach penile engorgement and–along with the less intense orgasm–they experience a lengthened refractory period during which an erection cannot be attained. Finally, long periods of celibacy can lead to some atrophy in the sexual organs. The most common misunderstanding aging men have is their need for more intense stimulation to achieve erection and ejaculation. Men often misunderstand this normal change and think they are becoming impotent (Fazio, 1988). Older women do experience some physiological changes (see Table 7.1). They also experience slower and less intense arousal. There is a reduction in the volume of lubricating fluid and a thinning of vaginal walls. However, a woman's orgasm remains unaffected by aging changes.

In the past two decades, researchers have focused on quantifying the sexual behavior of older adults (see Table 7.2). Pfeiffer (1974) reported on a ten-year longitudinal study of men. He compared sexual activity in the decade between 68 and 78 years of age. He reported that while 80% of men in both age groups continued to be interested in sex, sexual activity declined significantly. Seventy-eight percent of 68-year-olds were sexually active, whereas only 25% of 78-year-olds were. A second important association was also noted: sexual activity in later years was highly related to sexual interest and expression in early years.

Martin (1981) also conducted a longitudinal study of men 60-79 years old. Of his original sample of 188 married men, 56 were re-interviewed seven years later (and all were still married). He divided his sample into the most and least sexually active members and compared them. Martin, consistent with Pfeiffer's report (1974), found that there was a strong relationship between the level of activity in the men's younger years and their level of sexual activity in older age. A large proportion of the least active group (30%) reported problems with premature ejaculation and erectile failure. Interestingly, there were no differences between the groups in terms of marital satisfaction.

George and Weiler (1981) conducted the largest longitudinal study on sexual behavior in the elderly. Initially, they interviewed 502 men and women aged 46-71 and followed up with three surveys spread out every two years. Two hundred and seventy-eight respondents remained married throughout the study. Over the six-year study period, the mean level of sexual activity remained stable. Stable activity was reported by 58% of the sample; 20% decreased their activity; 5% increased their activity; and 7% were inactive all six years. Men consistently reported higher levels of sexual activity than did women, and younger cohorts reported higher levels than older ones. Cessation of sexual activity was linked to the attitudes

TABLE 7.2. Sexual Activity in Married Community Elderly

Study	Findings
<u>Martin (1981)</u> Longitudinal study of married men	•most active sexually in older age were the most active in younger years. •least active had problems with premature ejaculation and erectile failure.
<u>George & Weiler (1981)</u> Longitudinal study of married men and women	•level of sexual acitivity remained stable over a six year period. •men reported increased level of sexual activity vs. women. •cessation linked to attitudes of male partner.
<u>Pfeiffer (1974)</u> Longitudinal study of men	•sexual activity decreased significantly between ages 68-78.

of the male partner. Once again, sexual behavior during the study period was highly related to past sexual behavior.

Starr (1981) criticized the focus on quantifying sexual behavior of the elderly without exploring the qualitative meaning elderly gave to their sexual behavior. Comfort (1974), for example, described sexuality in the elderly as a solace, a source of self-esteem. Starr provided data on those qualitative aspects, asking older respondents to write answers to a 50-item open-ended questionnaire. Seventy-five percent of respondents stated that sex in older age feels as good or better than when they were younger. Ninety-five percent stated they liked sex, and 99% wanted sex. Forty-six percent masturbated, and 93% regarded touching and cuddling as important. Seventy-six percent felt that sex had a positive effect on their health. Interestingly, other authors have noted the beneficial effects of sex. Martin (1981) reported in his sample that 69% felt sex was important for good health. Andrews (1988) reviewed evidence that sexually active men slept better and were more cognitively able than inactive men.

In summary, the data indicate that older adults lead active, satisfying sex lives. While sexual activity unquestionably decreased in the "old old," this may be due to a cohort effect rather than the effect of aging. Indeed, despite the list of physiological changes in older age, the experience of sex does not appear to diminish. The level of sexual activity appears to be highly related to sexual behavior throughout adulthood. In the next section, reasons for decreased sexual activity in the aged will be analyzed.

REASONS FOR DECREASED SEXUALITY IN THE AGED

A number of psychosocial and medical factors lead to decreased sexuality. Sexual decline in the aged is most typically due to the male partner (George and Weiler, 1981; Schover, 1985). Martin (1981) described three processes in men that lead to sexual apathy. First, in those men with a life history of low sexual activity , a minor loss in motivation can cause them to stop being sexual. Second, social isolation often leads to cessation of sexual behavior. Finally, men may become unresponsive to stimuli that previously evoked erotic reactions. Masters and Johnson (1981) linked social dysfunction to the "widower's syndrome." This syndrome refers to men whose wives are suffering from a long-term illness. During the illness, there are no sexual experiences. At a later time, when attempting to become sexually active again, the man cannot achieve an erection.

Major health problems are the most likely reasons for decreased sexual functioning (Andrews, 1988; Brower and Tanner, 1979; Masters and Johnson, 1981; Pfeiffer, 1974; Renshaw, 1985; Schover, 1985). Many of the common ailments likely to disrupt sexual functioning are listed in Table 7.3. Pfeiffer (1974) urged health professionals to view diseases in the elderly as only temporary interruptions, rather than causes for permanent cessation, of sexual expression.

Different authors focused on the effects of different diseases. Schover (1985) stated that vascular insufficiency is the most common cause of erection problems in men over 50. She pointed out, too, that medications such as anti-hypertension and antidepressants

TABLE 7.3. Major Health Problems Likely to Disrupt Sexual Functioning

Vascular Insufficiency

Spinal Cord Injuries

Prostate Problems

Heart Disease

Incontinence

Diabetes

Respiratory Illness

Depression

Alcohol Abuse

Medications

can have effects on sexual functioning. Brower and Tanner (1979) noted that when an older adult is ill, strength is limited and fatigability lowers one's motivation to engage in sexual activities. Cardiovascular, respiratory, and neurological diseases were highlighted, as were alcohol, sedatives, and hypertensives.

Andrews reviewed the effects of diabetes, incontinence, heart disease, and depression on sexual functioning. Diabetes can lead to erectile impotence due to neuropathy. In women, itching and infections can make intercourse painful. Incontinence, a major problem in long-term-care-elderly, also leads to decreased sexual functioning. Angina, which can cause pain while engaging in sexual intercourse, also leads to decreased sexual activity. Renshaw (1985) noted that 10%-30% of men who undergo prostatectomy surgery have retrograde ejaculation due to internal bladder sphincter damage.

INTERVENTIONS FOR SEXUAL DYSFUNCTION

Schover (1985) provided an in-depth review of the treatment options offered to older adults with sexual dysfunction. The monitoring of natural erections has been the most accepted diagnostic test. A relatively inexpensive "snap gauge," which breaks during a rigid erection, has at times been utilized in place of more extensive monitoring equipment. Schover, however, pointed out that rarely do older adults seek treatment. Only 3% of Johns Hopkins sex-clinic patients were over 60 during a ten-year span, and none was over 70.

Indeed, programs to educate or even study sexuality have met with strong resistance in many elderly. Brower and Tanner (1979) found that many elders were angered and embarrassed during a sex education program for the elderly. Indeed, only 13% of the sample that took the pretest filled out the posttest after a two-session program. Wasow and Loeb (1979) found that 50% of those older adults approached refused to complete a confidential survey on their sexual behavior. Sexuality, and sexual dysfunction, remain taboo subjects to many elderly.

SEXUAL ACTIVITY IN LONG-TERM CARE

This section will review studies on the amount of elderly sexual activity, how sexuality can be best assessed, and the dilemmas that long-term-care staff must face. Later, staff attitudes toward sexuality in long-term-care patients will be reviewed. A critique of the existing literature will then be presented. This will be followed by presenting a novel, practical method of assessing the appropriateness of partnered sexual activity in patients. Case studies will be used to illustrate the assessment.

There have only been a few empirical studies on sexual behavior in long-term care (Kaas, 1978; Szasz, 1983; Wasow and Loeb, 1979 and 1980; and White, 1982a). A summary of these studies can be found in Table 7.4. Wasow and Loeb interviewed 27 men and 36 women in long-term care, and a large concentration of their respondents was over age 85. Ten percent of the sample participated in sexual intercourse and 10% reported masturbating. Almost 70% of men admitted to sexual thoughts, whereas only 25% of women did. The majority of men (58%) and women (78%) felt unattractive. Finally, not having a partner, poor health, or lack of interest were the most common reasons for sexual inactivity. These data were consistent with Kassel's argument (1983) that many long-term-care

TABLE 7.4. Sexual Activity in Long-Term Care

Study	Findings
Kaas (1978)	•61% of patients did not feel sexually attractive •lack of privacy seen as most important factor in limiting sexuality
Wasow & Loeb (1979, 1980) Interviewed 27 males, 35 females in 1 long term care facility	•10% participated in sexual intercourse •10% masturbated •males reported more sexual fantasies
White (1982) Stratified random sample in 15 long term care facilities. Interviewed 84 males, 185 females with ASKAS Scale	•8% stated they were sexually active •17% stated an interest in being sexually active •sexual interest was highly related to current sexual activity
Szasz (1983) Surveyed 83 staff in 1 long term care facility to determine male residents' sexual behavior	•35 incidents of sexual talk •71 incidents of sexual acts •5 incidents of implied sexual behavior •25% sample stated public masturbation as the most bothersome event •private masturbation permitted by 12% of sample

patients have a major lack of sexual interest due to illness and overmedication.

White (1982b) utilized a stratified random sample in 15 long-term care facilities in deriving his sample of 84 men and 185 women (see Table 7.4). Men had an average age of 81 years and women an average age of 83 years. Seventy-five percent of those approached agreed to participate. Respondents were interviewed in private, and the interview included the Aging Sexuality Knowledge and Attitudes Scale (ASKAS). The ASKAS contains 30 questions dealing with sexual attitudes. The results were consistent with that of Wasow and Loeb. Eight percent of the sample were sexually active. A slightly higher number of respondents, 17%, stated that they were interested in being sexually active but lacked the opportunity. In the study, sexual knowledge and sexual attitudes were unrelated. Unfortunately, the author did not analyze the results with respect to gender and, thus, no separate information was provided for men and women.

Szasz (1983) approached patient sexual activity in long-term care by surveying the staff in a 400-bed facility for men. Data were provided by 71 staff (not 83, as Szasz claimed); 16 RNs, 25 LPNs, 26 NAs and 4 orderlies (for a 78% return rate). One hundred and twenty-three sexual incidents were cited as problematic, and these were divided into three categories (see Table 7.4). Sexual talk, sexual acts, and implied sexual behavior were cited. Sexual talk ranged from patients discussing their own sexual problems to requesting sex with staff. Sexual acts included exposing themselves, grabbing private parts of others, and masturbating publicly. Public masturbation was the most bothersome event. Hugging staff and private masturbation were viewed as acceptable.

These studies demonstrate that sexual activity is clearly present in long-term-care patients. Yet it remains a neglected topic. One reason for its neglect is that few tests have been developed to help assess the elderly patient's sexual knowledge and attitudes. The ASKAS will be reviewed here in order to provide information on the scale's reliability and validity (White, 1982b). The ASKAS was created for use in long-term care. The 30 knowledge questions on the ASKAS cover such things as the decrease in firmness of the older male's erection; reduced vaginal lubrication in older women; and slowed sexual response time. Attitude questions are answered on a Likert scale, with answers ranging from "strongly agree" to "strongly disagree." These include such items as "aged people with sexual interest bring disgrace"; "long-term care should not support sexual activity"; and "long-term care should provide privacy for patients to engage in sexual behavior."

Evidence for reliability and validity for the ASKAS is quite strong. Using nine different samples, White (1982) found such reliability coefficients as split-half, alpha, and test-retest to be in the acceptable range with most scores above the 0.85 level. Evidence for the scale's validity was also provided. In one study, an experimental group of older adults exposed to sex education showed a significantly improved knowledge score on the ASKAS, whereas the control group did not. Similar findings were reported for groups of long-term-care staff and for mental-health professionals who work with the elderly. White (1982b) argued that the ASKAS can be used routinely in long-term care to assess sexuality in older adults.

The research has presented sexuality in long-term care with clinical objectivity. Implicitly, it is recommended that those who want to be sexually active should be allowed or encouraged to do so. Kassel (1983) suggested that medication and families' adverse reactions are the only reasons why sexual expression is stifled in long-term care. The reality of long-term care is much more complex, however, and there are dilemmas these authors did not illuminate. These will be explored here. Following that, the focus will shift to long-term-care staff attitudes toward sexuality in patients.

McCartney et al. (1987) compared and contrasted the acceptance of sexuality in long-term care patients when the patients were demented and when they were not. In one case, a 72-year-old non-demented widower engaged in a relationship with a non-demented woman. They openly hugged and kissed. The staff approved of this relationship and gave the couple a DO NOT DISTURB sign to use when they shared a room. However, when a 79-year-old Alzheimer's patient became sexually interested in a demented woman, the staff became upset and set firm limits with him. McCartney concluded that long-term-care facilities act in a parental manner with regard to demented patients and seek to control their behavior. There was no determination of the patients' competency to understand, to consent to, or to form a relationship. Before addressing this dilemma further, staff attitudes toward sexuality will be reviewed (see Table 7.5).

As can be seen in Table 7.5, the empirical evidence does not lend total support to the views expressed by Falk and Falk (1980) and Kassel (1983). In an early study on staff attitudes, Kaas compared 85 long-term-care residents with 207 staff from four facilities. In-

TABLE 7.5. Staff Attitudes Toward Sexuality in Long-Term-Care Facilities

Study	Findings
<u>Falk & Falk (1980)</u> <u>Kassel (1983)</u> Clinical observations from their consulting practices	•long term care facilities refuse to accept sexuality in patients •most common reason for requested transfer is the patient engaging in masturbation
<u>Glass, Mustian & Carter (1986)</u> 57 Staff from 5 skilled nursing facilities. Gave sample the ASKAS scale	•persons who had higher level knowledge had more restrictive scores •persons with greater nursing education had more permissive attitudes
<u>Wasow & Loeb (1979; 1980)</u> Interviewed 62 patients and 17 staff in one long term care facility	•authors met significant resistance from administrators in conducting study. •staff had more permissive attitudes toward sexuality than did the patients
<u>Kaas (1978)</u> Questionnaire to 85 patients and 207 staff in 5 long term care facilities	•staff had significantly more permissive attitudes toward sexual expression than did the patients
<u>White & Catania (1982)</u> Psycho-educational intervention with 30 long term care staff experimental v. control group	•long term care experimental group showed increased sexual knowledge following intervention •long term care experimental group showed increased permissive attitudes following intervention
<u>Damrosch (1982; 1984)</u> Had 260 undergraduate nursing students, 114 graduate student nurses rate vignettes	•both samples rated the sexually active long term care person significantly higher in cheerfulness, mental alertness, adjustment, etc.

terestingly, the staff had significantly more permissive attitudes about sexuality in the elderly than did the elderly themselves.

Wasow and Loeb (1979, 1980) encountered a variety of staff attitudes when completing their study of 62 patients and 17 staff. First, administrators were very resistant to allowing them to complete the study. Upon interviewing their sample, however, they also found that the staff had a permissive attitude, whereas patients, overall, had a very restrictive attitude toward sexual expression.

Glass, Mustian, and Carter (1986) had 57 RNs, LPNs, and NAs from five long-term-care facilities complete the ASKAS scale. The mean knowledge score was in the moderately knowledgeable range, and the mean attitude score was in the highly restrictive range. There was a significant inverse correlation between the knowledge scores and attitude scores ($r = 0.30$). As knowledge about elders' sexuality increased, attitudes became more restrictive. In a separate analysis, however, it was found that persons with greater nursing education had more permissive attitudes. Interpretation of these results suggested that LPNs and NAs had the most restrictive attitudes and that these attitudes were not lessened through increased education.

White and Catania's study (1982) included 30 long-term-care staff and found exactly the opposite of Glass, Mustian, and Carter (1986). Compared with a control group, an experimental group that received a psycho-educational program significantly improved their knowledge and significantly changed their attitude in a more permissive direction. Clearly, these two studies do not provide conclusive information. They do, however, serve to make all aware of the divergence in opinions regarding sexuality in the older long-term-care patient.

Damrosch (1982, 1984) described two studies that measured the sexual attitudes of undergraduate nursing students and graduate student nurses. In the first study, 206 undergraduate students read a vignette about a 68-year-old woman in a long-term-care facility. One half read that the woman was sexually active, while the other half read a passage that did not mention sexuality. The sexually active adult was viewed more positively. In the second study, 114 graduate student nurses (90% of whom worked full time as an RN) read the vignette about the 68-year-old woman in long-term care.

This time, marital status and sexuality were varied. While there was only one main effect for marital status (increased family warmth), the sexually active person received significantly higher scores on nine of ten items (e.g., alertness, cheerfulness, etc.). Damrosch (1984) offered three explanations for her findings: There may be increasingly liberal attitudes toward sexuality in the aged; the results may be due to sample bias; or "atypical" elderly may be evaluated more positively.

In reviewing the studies, it is clear that the evidence is equivocal. Some researchers found staff to be permissive, while others found them to be restrictive. In some studies, knowledge and attitudes were directly related; in other studies, they were inversely related. Methodological reasons may account for some of the large discrepancy in findings. The staff that filled out the surveys may be a select group, and they may differ from nonparticipating staff in that their views (tolerant or intolerant) may be more extreme. In addition, general staff attitudes about sexuality may not capture beliefs about specific situations involving sexuality in long-term care. There are also several shortcomings in the present conceptualization of sexuality in long-term-care aged. The question of should elderly patients be allowed sexual expression needs to be changed to a question of under what circumstances and conditions should elderly patients be allowed and/or encouraged to pursue sexual relationships. In none of the studies measuring quantity of sexual behavior in long-term care did the researchers address the distinction between cognitively intact and demented patients. In none of the staff attitude studies was the impact of cognitive impairment addressed. Note that Damrosch's (1982, 1984) 68-year-old patient is similar to McCartney's (1987) case study of sanctioned sexuality. Both were cognitively intact.

A major concern in long-term care is that a dementia patient not be subject to exploitation. A sexually aggressive demented man, for example, may be permitted to engage in sex with a demented older woman solely because she believes that he is her husband. Unfortunately, as McCartney (1987) points out, staff are typically very restrictive with demented patients, and they constrain them without even assessing their ability to consent to a relationship. This practice is entirely too prohibitive. What follows is a model of assessing demented patients' ability to participate in sexual relationships.

ASSESSING DEMENTED PATIENTS

Lichtenberg and Strzepek (1990) described a procedure that could help long-term-care professionals assess patients' competencies to participate in intimate, sexual relationships. Collopy (1988) outlined three necessary conditions for informed consent. First, the behavior must be judged to be an authentic choice. Second, the participant must have mental competence. Collopy urged the avoidance of global judgment about competency. He instead stated the need to recognize the context-specific nature of competency. Third, the patient must be aware of risks and benefits.

Sexuality is one of the earliest learned behaviors. In observing mixed sex groups of demented individuals, these old learned social and sex-role behaviors are quite apparent. Sexuality, as an earlier section noted, is a reality in long-term care. What, then, is the best way to determine who is competent and who is not? The following method of assessment has been utilized in 15 cases. It is still an evolving method, but one that has been useful. As can be seen in Table 7.6, the assessment has two possible components–cognitive screening and an extended interview. The assessment is analyzed in a decision-tree format. A certain amount of cognitive abilities are necessary for competence. The Mini Mental State Exam is given, and a cut-off score of 14 is utilized. If the patient scores above 14 points on the exam, the extended interview is conducted by a same-sex interviewer.

The first area of the interview is the patient's awareness of the relationship. The following questions are good openings for discussion: Is the patient aware of who the other person is? Do they believe that the other person is a spouse, for example, and thus acquiesce? Is the patient aware of who is initiating sexual contact (they or their sexual partner)? Can the patient state what level of intimacy they would be comfortable with?

The second area explored is the patient's ability to avoid exploitation: Is the behavior consistent with formerly held beliefs or

TABLE 7.6. Decision Tree for Assessing Competency to Participate in an Intimate Relationship

<u>Mini Mental State Score Greater than 14</u>

Yes	No
Perform assessment interview	Patient unable to consent

<u>Patient's ability to avoid exploitation</u>

Yes	No
Continue evaluation	Patient unable to consent

<u>Patient's awareness of the relationship</u>

Yes	No
Continue evaluation	Patient unable to consent

<u>Patient's awareness of risk</u>

Yes	No
Consider patient competent to participate in an intimate relationship	Provide frequent reminders of risks but permit relationship

values? Does the patient have the capacity to say no to any uninvited sexual contact?

In the final area, the patient's awareness of potential risks are explored: Does the patient realize that this relationship may be time-limited? Can the patient describe how they will react when the relationship ends?

The interview material is then analyzed as follows. First, patients must be protected from exploitation. Thus, if the patient appears unable to set the limits with their partner, or feels that they must always submit to sexual demands, then they are judged not competent. Next, the patient's awareness of the relationship is analyzed. Delusional beliefs that their partner is a long-term spouse, or denial that any relationship exists, demonstrate a lack of awareness. Patients must be aware of the relationship to make competent decisions. Finally, awareness of risk is analyzed. Note that awareness of risk is not necessary for allowing intimate relationships (Table 7.6). It is important, however, to assess and, if need be, provide frequent reminders regarding potential risks.

The results of the expanded interview are relayed to the interdisciplinary team. Team members provide feedback on any behavioral evidence that supported or contradicted the patient's responses. From these data, decisions are made regarding the patient's competence to participate in an intimate relationship.

Family involvement is a necessary and sometimes difficult process. When patients are found competent, and they will be engaging in a romantic relationship, the family is contacted. They are brought up to date on their family member's sexual interests, and their own views on sexuality are explored. The assessment process is explained and the results discussed. When the family has concerns, they should be invited to discuss these with the treatment team. However, unless the family can share behavioral observations that contradict the assessment findings, the team will allow the romantic relationship to continue. The following case examples illustrate how the assessment process can work.

Case 1

A demented, widowed woman in her 70s, depressed and still grieving the loss of her husband ten years earlier, began to perk up when she became the object of a 70-year-old male's attention. The man had been married three times and had the reputation of being a ladies' man. At the beginning of the relationship, both patients seemed happier and could be seen walking up and down the halls arm in arm; they kissed and fondled as well. Both expressed great pleasure in the relationship. She said he filled an "empty place" in her heart, and he repeatedly stated what a "fine" woman she was. They also spent a lot of time talking to each other and clearly enjoyed a social relationship.

On the Mini Mental State Exam, he had a score of 20 and she a score of 21. During an interview, both patients appeared to be cognizant of the identity and intent of the other. He wished for intercourse, but she did not. It was clear that she could say no to unwanted sexual contact (and had in fact done so) and that he respected her limits. She was also capable of saying she did not want to get in too deep and get hurt. He was clear about his wishes and also realized the relationship might not last. The staff agreed that they were competent and allowed them sexual contact within the limits set by the couple.

Case 2

In this case, a sexual relationship was denied between a married couple. Mr. M. was a 78-year-old retired accountant, and his wife was a 74-year-old retired custodial worker. The couple met after Mr. M.'s 30-year marriage ended after he was widowed. For the first four years of their marriage, their relationship was a good one. She then, however, became demented. He, in turn, became angry and physically abusive toward her. As her dementia increased, he also became mildly demented. Social services responded to many complaints from their neighbors, but could not be awarded guardian status by the courts. Finally, due to neglect, Mrs. M. was hospitalized and later sent to long-term care. Mr. M. also entered long-term care a year later, when social services was awarded guardianship.

Mr. M. resumed his abusive pattern toward his wife. She, in turn, was compliant to all of his demands; her behavior deteriorated, however. She was uncooperative with staff and depressed. Mini Mental State Scores were 22 for Mr. M and 8 for Mrs. M. During the interview, it was clear that Mrs. M. could not avoid exploitation (she privately stated that she did not want a sexual relationship with her husband). Mr. M., interestingly, confided that although he had engaged in sexual relations with his wife in long-term care, he was not eager to continue this practice. Due to Mrs. M.'s incompetence, the staff agreed to monitor the couple and prevent sexual intercourse.

SUMMARY

Sexuality in long-term care is a topic that has only recently received research and clinical attention. Sexual behavior research has demonstrated some converging trends. First, a significant minority of patients are sexually active in long-term care. Second, attitudes toward sexuality are varied. Some long-term-care staff are tolerant of sexuality in their patients and others are blatantly intolerant. However, the patients-particularly the demented patients-have not been allowed to give their input into their own choice of sexual expression. Without even assessing the patient's competency, staff constrain demented patients. This chapter offers a method of assessing demented patient's ability to comprehend their sexual activity and choose their sexual partner.

REFERENCES

Andrews, J. (1988). The Effects of Poor Health on Sexual Activity. *Geriatric Nursing and Home Care, February,* 17.

Brower, H.T., and Tanner, L.A. (1979). A Study of Older Adults Attending a Program on Human Sexuality: A Pilot Study. *Nursing Research, 28,* 36-39.

Collopy, B. (1988). Autonomy in Long Term Care: Some Crucial Distinctions. *The Gerontologist, 28,* 10-18.

Comfort A. (1974). Sexuality in Old Age. *Journal of the American Geriatrics Society, 22,* 440-442.

Damrosch, S. (1982). Nursing Students' Attitudes Toward Sexually Active Older Persons. *Nursing Research, 31,* 252-255.

Damrosch, S.P. (1984). Graduate Nursing Students' Attitudes Toward Sexually Active Older Persons. *The Gerontologist, 24,* 299-302.

Falk, G., and Falk, U.A. (1980). Sexuality and the Aged. *Nursing Outlook, January,* 51-55.

Fazio, L. (1988). Sexuality and Aging: A Community Wellness Program. *Physical and Occupational Therapy in Geriatrics,* 59-69.

George, L.K., and Weiler, S.J. (1981). Sexuality in Middle and Late Life. *Archives of General Psychiatry, 38,* 919-923.

Glass, J.C., Mustian, R.D., and Carter, L.R. (1986). Knowledge and Attitudes of Health Care Providers Toward Sexuality in the Institutionalized Elderly. *Educational Gerontology, 12,* 465- 475.

Kaas, M.J. (1978). Sexual Expression of the Elderly in Nursing Homes. *The Gerontologist, 18,* 372-378.

Kassel, V. (1983). Long-Term Care Institutions. In Weg, R. (ed.), *Sexuality in the Later Years.* Academic Press: New York, pp. 167-184.

Lichtenberg, P.A., and Strzepek, D.M. (1990). Assessments of Institutionalized Dementia Patients' Competencies to Participate in Intimate Relationships. *The Gerontologist, 30,* 117-119.

Ludeman, K. (1981). The Sexuality of the Older Person: Review of the Literature. *The Gerontologist, 21,* 203-208.

Martin, C.E. (1981). Factors Affecting Sexual Functioning in 60-79-Year-Old Married Males. *Archives of Sexual Behavior, 10,* 399-420.

Masters, W.H., and Johnson, V.E. (1981). Sex and the Aging Process. *Journal of the American Geriatrics Society, 29,* 385-390.

McCartney, J.R., Izeman, H., Rogers, D., and Cohen, N. (1987). Sexuality and the Institutionalized Elderly. *Journal of the American Geriatrics Society, 35,* 331-333.

Pfeiffer, E. (1974). Sexuality in the Aging Individual. *Journal of the American Geriatrics Society, 22,* 481-484.

Renshaw, D.C. (1985). Sex, Age, and Values. *Journal of the American Geriatrics Society, 33,* 635-643.

Schover, L.R. (1985). Sexual Problems. In Teri, L., and Lewinsohn, P. (eds.), *Geropsychological Assessment and Treatment.* Springer Publishing Co.: New York.

Starr, B.D. (1981). *The Starr-Weiner Report on Sex and Sexuality in the Mature Years.* McGraw Hill: New York.

Steinke, E.E., and Bergen, M.B. (1984). Sexuality and Aging. *Journal of Gerontological Nursing, 12,* 6-10.

Szasz, G. (1983). Sexual Incidents in an Extended Care Unit for Aged Men. *Journal of the American Geriatrics Society, 31,* 407-411.

Wasow, M., and Loeb, M.B. (1979). Sexuality in Nursing Homes. *Journal of the American Geriatrics Society, 27,* 73-79.

Wasow, M., and Loeb, M.B. (1980). Sexuality in Nursing Homes. In Solnick, R. (ed.), *Sexuality and Aging.* University of Southern California Press: Los Angeles. pp. 154-162.

White, C.B. (1982a). Sexual Interest, Attitudes, Knowledge, and Sexual History in Relation to Sexual Behavior in the Institutionalized Aged. *Archives of Sexual Behavior, 11,* 11-21.

White, C.B. (1982b). A Scale for the Assessment of Attitudes and Knowledge Regarding Sexuality in the Aged. *Archives of Sexual Behavior, 11,* 491-502.

White, C.B., and Catania, J.A. (1982). Psychoeducational Intervention for Sexuality with the Aged, Family Members of the Aged, and People Who Work with the Aged. *International Journal of Aging and Human Development, 15,* 121-138.

Chapter 8

Psychotherapy: Practical Applications in Geriatric Long-Term Care

This chapter is intended to be a companion to all of the treatment strategies detailed previously. The major focus will be on delineating major issues involved in psychotherapy for long-term patients. These major issues are: (1) the reluctance of psychotherapists to work with the elderly; (2) defining the long-term-care population; (3) embracing the patient's need for grief work in treating depression; and (4) varying one's therapeutic intervention depending on the patient's strengths.

RELUCTANCE OF PSYCHOTHERAPISTS

Psychotherapeutic work with the elderly, particularly the long-term-care elderly, has long been shunned by mental-health professionals (Lawton and Gottesman, 1974; Mintz, Steuer, and Jarvik, 1981; Rubin, 1977; Sparacino, 1979; and Williams, 1989). Many reasons for this professional ageism have been cited and most focus on the inability of the professional to "master" chronic conditions in the elderly. Sparacino (1979) cited four reasons why professionals shy away from treating the elderly: (1) they feel powerless because they believe they cannot treat the organic states in elders; (2) the desire to avoid "wasting" skills on those nearing death; (3) fear that the patient may die during treatment; and (4) an "over-identification" with physically ill elders. Lawton and Gottesman (1974) attributed therapists' reluctance to unresolved conflicts with parental images and the need to deny their own mortality. Williams (1989) echoed these sentiments and expanded upon why professionals avoid working with bereaved elderly. First, the therapists are confronted by their own powerlessness. Second, they are fearful of exploring their own history of losses. Finally, therapists are uncomfortable with the need to draw close to the dying in order to discover their needs.

The lack of research on psychotherapy with the elderly also reflects its low status in the mental-health professions. Sparacino (1979) concluded that published research on the topic has been infrequent and methodologically weak, and that clinical reports were vague. Mintz, Steuer, and Jarvik (1981) cited a number of psychotherapy variables yet to be investigated. These included heterogeneity in the elderly, physical illness and depression, modalities of treatment, therapist's experience and attitude, therapist's age, reliability of measures, and followup information.

Rubin (1977) cited direct, supervised experience as the best way to overcome reluctance in providing psychotherapy for the elderly. Indeed, in the last decade more professionals in training are having direct therapy experience with the elderly. This has led to an increased interest in the field and to valuable new resources (Knight, 1985; Teri and Lewinsohn, 1986). Still, psychotherapy with long-term-care elders remains in its infancy. Given that a thorough neuropsychological assessment from a mental-health worker (or other team member) uncovers psychological problems in the patient, how does one proceed?

Seeing Past the Deficit Model

Problems, such as with affect, behavior, or cognition, present themselves as deficits. Something is lacking (e.g., happiness in a depressed patient) and needs to be corrected. It is vital, however, that before beginning treatment for this deficit, the therapist consider the patient's strengths. Older adults are survivors, and although they may be coping poorly at present, it is important to discover their successful coping skills from the past. Illnesses, such as physical conditions, depression, and dementia are chronic conditions. What has the older patient done in the past to accommodate these conditions? In physically ill patients, cognitive and social skills may be areas of strength. In mentally ill patients, hobbies may represent strengths. In dementia patients, some areas of cognition may be relative strengths, and social or recreational skills often remain as strengths. Aging is not all decline. As Butler (1974) pointed out, there are many myths about aging. Some myths are that aging consistently produces unproductivity, disengagement, inflexibility, senility, or serenity. The aged are as diverse a group as any, and individual strengths must be an inherent part of psychotherapeutic treatment.

DEFINING THE LONG-TERM-CARE POPULATION

The three major patient groups needing psychotherapy in long-term care are the physically ill, but cognitively capable; the mentally ill, but cognitively capable; and the demented. Different therapeutic issues arise and different interventions are needed for each group. This distinction, however, has rarely been made in the clinical literature. Barns, Sack, and Shore (1973) identified two of these as "mind twist" and "mind loss," but recommended the same treatment for each. Listed below are some of the tasks that each long-term-care elderly patient must face. These include:

- Making a transition into the facility
- Establishing relationships with staff
- Adapting to the institution's schedule
- Adjusting to new roles with family caregivers or to a lack of family caregivers
- Accommodating to a new activities schedule

GRIEF WORK IN TREATING DEPRESSION

Patients who have difficulty with one or more of the above-stated tasks display them in different ways. Grief and depression, prominent problems in long-term-care patients, are exhibited differently by patients and are dealt with differently in psychotherapy, depending on the patient's capabilities. Brink (1985) identified depression, hypochondriasis, and paranoia as frequent reactions to grief. Williams (1989) echoed the belief that loss and bereavement are ever present in the elderly. Four common abnormal grieving patterns were identified: (1) chronic grief, (2) delayed grief, (3) exaggerated grief (i.e., depression), and (4) repressed grief. How, then, are grief and depression exhibited and treated differently, given the patient's capabilities?

THE VARYING THERAPEUTIC INTERVENTIONS: GRIEF, LOSS, AND DEPRESSION IN THE PHYSICALLY ILL ELDERLY

Elderly women suffering from a number of painful chronic diseases such as arthritis, gout, and osteoporosis make up a large proportion of these patients. Several characteristics are common in the subgroup of these patients; members of this subgroup often become clinically depressed upon entering long-term care. Grief, it must be understood, does not occur in a vacuum. A loss such as the loss of independent living or of a free existence stirs up previous losses. Each major loss thus provokes emotional reactions about previous losses that may yet be unresolved. A common pattern of losses has been noted:

• Major early-life losses
• Loss of intimacy due to history of sexual, physical, or emotional abuse
• Loss of self-esteem due to passive interpersonal style

These patients, however, have often led successful, productive lives and have the cognitive abilities to engage in intensive psychotherapy. Several excellent methods of treatment include life review (Butler, 1974); symbolic giving (Yesavage and Karasu, 1982), successful dependency (Goldfarb, 1952); and cognitive behavioral treatment (Knight, 1985; Thompson et al., 1986). Here, a technique will be described that utilizes many of these methods.

Mrs. D.

Mrs. D. was an 86-year-old divorced, retired telephone operator who fell in her apartment and fractured her right hip. A hip replacement was conducted, but Mrs. D. did not recover enough to return home. Instead, she entered long-term care. On a neuropsychological evaluation, Mrs. D. was found to have intact attention, language, and verbal reasoning. Consistent with advanced age, she showed some mild mental flexibility and memory deficits. On the Geriatric Depression Scale, however, Mrs. D. scored in the severely depressed range. She complained of feeling bored, empty, hopeless, blue, and worthless–with sleep and concentration problems and a poor appetite. She repeatedly thought about death. Psychotherapy was offered to Mrs. D., and she accepted the offer. Thompson et al. (1986) described the importance of educating elderly patients about psychotherapy. It is helpful to describe therapy as being similar to visiting a physician on one hand and to talking with a friend on the other. Mrs. D.'s immediate complaints centered around giving up her apartment and her family caregiver's treatment of her. The initial psychotherapy session was spent on learning how Mrs. D. perceived her problems. Mrs. D. was furious with her niece, who, when closing Mrs. D.'s apartment, gave away all of Mrs. D.'s belongings without asking Mrs. D. how she wanted to distribute her possessions. Mrs. D. had not discussed the matter directly with her niece because she feared that her niece would become angry. When asked how things could improve, Mrs. D. stated that her niece should realize her mistake and apologize. She viewed herself as powerless.

The second session is begun by directly confronting the often hidden and unrealistic expectations the patient holds about treatment. Mrs. D. was told that the therapist could not help her with one of her goals for treatment, changing her niece. Patients enter treatment believing that their depression would subside if only a significant other would change. It is important to confront this issue and to illustrate how little we all are able to control or change another person's behavior. Second, Mrs. D. was confronted with the fact that, despite her feelings of powerlessness, she blamed herself for the negative events in her life. In order to progress in treatment, she was told that she would have to address this issue in therapy. Mrs. D. was terribly critical of herself. At the end of this session, Mrs. D. was then offered possible treatment goals. These included helping her depression and self-esteem by making changes in herself. At this time, Mrs. D. was again offered psychotherapy. Since control and choice have been shown to be such powerful correlates of positive adaptation in long-term care (Langer and Rodin, 1976; Schulz, 1976), it is important to once again offer psychotherapy. This time, however, the focus is on realistic goals.

Mrs. D. began to experience the pain of her recent losses when she discussed early-childhood losses. Her mother died when she was nine. Her father, an alcoholic, remarried when she was 13. He never complimented her and rarely paid any attention to her. Her stepmother viewed her as a nuisance. Here, anger and sadness were identified for Mrs. D. as normal and acceptable emotions. While in her forties, Mrs. D. married. Desperate to combat her loneliness, she married an alcoholic who physically and sexually abused her. She summoned the courage to leave him, but lost all self-esteem. It was important to label the above incidents as abusive and in no way acceptable.

Therapeutic interventions and interpretations can come early in treatment with many geriatric patients. Although she had never discussed any of the above, it is clear that past losses were impacting on her transition to long-term care. She had suffered minor depression much of her life, and exploration of her emotional pain was not difficult once it was encouraged.

Therapy should connect past losses and coping styles and apply them to the present situation. Although for Mrs. D., it was probably adaptive to avoid verbal confrontations with her father and her husband, it was not necessarily useful to avoid confronting her niece. Mrs. D. was hurt and angry. She was encouraged to explore what she wanted from her niece, how she could ask for it, and how she could discuss her present anger. She was hesitant to confront her niece.

Mrs. D. pursued improving her relationship with her niece by asking her niece to visit at certain times and for specific events. Much time was spent in therapy challenging her harsh criticisms of herself, and she began to smile and to laugh more. Her major depression subsided. She continued to struggle with some dysphoria, and time was spent on improving her assertiveness skills. She continued to value psychotherapy and to work on these lifelong issues of loss. She learned that she would still retain the emotional scars of abuse, but that she could live an enriched life as well.

Many points that were integral to Mrs. D.'s treatments can be extrapolated to the psychotherapeutic treatment of other physically ill, cognitively able patients. First, it is necessary to discover the patient's original expectations for therapy and to confront impossible goals. Second, elderly patients need to be introduced to the basic rules of psychotherapy and how the relationship is a unique one. The patient must control therapy, in that they must agree to the psychotherapy and to the goals that are set. Otherwise, if they do not agree, therapy should be terminated. Third, exploration of current grief leads to unresolved past losses. Many of these losses, such as physical or sexual abuse, have never been discussed. Reminiscence often takes the form of grief work. Fourth, extremely useful skills can be taught, such as assertiveness and anger management.

PSYCHOTHERAPY WITH MENTALLY ILL ELDERLY

Mentally ill elders, such as those suffering from schizophrenia or bipolar disease, have often spent many years in institutions. Elders living in the 1990s have been in and out of hospitals. Indeed, in contrast to past cohorts of mentally ill (who often lived most of their lives in a single hospital), this current cohort of patients faces numerous relocations. Throughout the country, state hospitals have closed geriatric programs and transferred the patients to various long-term-care settings. These mentally ill patients do not have the quality of coping skills that other patients have. Indeed, their grief during transition periods often takes the form of interpersonal conflicts with staff and other patients. The following case illustrates this.

The Case of Ms. A.

Ms. A. was a 66-year-old woman who had spent the last 30 years in various psychiatric hospitals due to bipolar illness. Ms. A. was born into a family of nine children. Her parents were quite wealthy, since her father was a corporate executive. Ms. A. stated, however, that she was verbally, physically, and sexually abused throughout her childhood and adolescence. At age 17, she was hit on the head by a rock, which resulted in her seizure disorder. She graduated from high school and attended college, but could not finish due to the seizure problems. She went to work as a secretary.

A decade later, Ms. A. began to display heightened aggressive behavior. She struck her brother with a poker and destroyed several pieces of furniture. She displayed alternating symptoms from euphoria with grandiosity to deep depression. She was hospitalized. Her behavior remained unstable for two decades. She did, however, became much calmer and was released to the community when a state hospital program closed.

For one year, Ms. A. managed to live in the community. She was, however, victimized many times. Finally, after one robbery Ms. A. became psychotic. A local hospital treated her and transferred her to a long-term-care facility. Ms. A. was fully able to perform her ADL skills in the long-term-care facility, but from the start, she was having severe interpersonal difficulties. She was hostile and angry with both the staff and other patients. It was decided that she should enter individual psychotherapy with the psychologist.

Neuropsychological testing revealed a woman with a wealth of cognitive strengths. These included a fund of knowledge, auditory attention, and verbal abstract reasoning. Verbal and visuospatial recall and tests of mental flexibility were moderately impaired. The results indicated that there was a cognitive decline consistent with a severe seizure disorder. On the Geriatric Depression Scale, Ms. A. scored in the range of moderate depression. She complained of feeling empty, blue, helpless, sleeping poorly, and overeating.

Ms. A. was told that psychotherapy would be a time to discuss her concerns, whatever they may be. The first goal in psychotherapy that was agreed upon was that Ms. A. should bring problematic events to the therapy session for discussion prior to sharing her concerns with others. Up to that point, Ms. A. expressed her feelings through indiscriminate angry tantrums. Later, she would feel guilty and attempt to make up with the staff she abused.

In therapy, persecutory themes permeated her description of the daily events in long-term care. She likened the staff, who acted in ways she did not always like, with her parents and siblings, who she believed had neglected and abandoned her. Depressive grief, related to her loss of health (physical and mental), and her loss of ambition (her goals) were most often expressed. Therapy was not used to confront her or her beliefs, but rather to help reduce her anger and to discuss ways of obtaining friendly reactions from others.

Ms. A. began to belittle the therapist and attempt to antagonize him as she became more involved in treatment. This reaction was also left unconfronted and uninterpreted. The therapist again attended to her feelings and validated that her concerns were important. At one point, Ms. A. quit therapy, claiming that her therapist did not stick up for her enough. After three weeks, she resumed treatment.

She then displayed an increased trust in the therapist. This was evidenced by enlisting the therapist's help in setting personal goals. She chose to engage in regular exercise, to resume reading, and to involve herself in recreational activities. She reduced her verbal altercations with the staff and patients by 80%. She increased the number of pleasant conversations she had. She became a helper to the recreational activities department and joined in with many of the programs. Ms. A.'s depression resolved, and she terminated treatment with the understanding that she had the control to resume it at any time.

The above case illustrates the reality of paranoid states in long-term-care patients. Berger and Zarit (1978) discussed how few attempts have been made at understanding and treating paranoid elderly. Whitbourne (1989) described the need to help the paranoid individual develop a sense of control. Basic strategies in psychotherapy with the major mentally ill are as follows. First, build trust through active listening. Second, limit or eliminate interpretations or confrontive statements, since these will likely be viewed by the patient as rejection. Third, allow the patient to express their hostility. Combat verbally abusive behavior with calm, assertive statements when necessary. Finally, allow the patient to determine the goals of therapy. As this case illustrated, the major goals of treatment are to engender trust. This trust will help reduce much of the intolerable behavior exhibited by the paranoid patient.

PSYCHOTHERAPY WITH THE DEMENTED

Several features distinguish psychotherapy with the demented from psychotherapy with the physically or mentally ill. The primary difference revolves around the ability to explicitly remember what was discussed. Recall of therapy content is obviously one of the cornerstones of traditional psychotherapy. Patients with moderate or advanced dementia cannot remember content from session to session. Behavioral psychotherapy, which focuses more on changing the environment than on changing personal beliefs, has recently been applied with the demented elderly.

Teri and Gallagher-Thompson (1991) and Teri and Logsdon (1991) have been among the first to focus upon individual treatment with demented patients. The authors extrapolated Lewinsohn's social learning theory to the moderately demented, depressed patient. The treatment strategy was to increase pleasant events so as to decrease the depression. Teri and Logsdon created a Pleasant Events Schedule for Alzheimer's disease patients to help identify pleasurable events for patients. Alzheimer's patients, they pointed out, often lose the ability to initiate activities that are rewarding and enjoyable. They listed 53 items, such as being outside, listening to music, being with pets, and receiving greeting cards. While their approach is extremely useful, it should not limit the therapy interventions.

Depressed, demented patients, such as those adjusting to long-term care, can benefit from the chance to express their grief in therapy. Typically, their grief is displayed as a general behavioral disturbance. That is, they are complaining, uncooperative, and resistive. Though their cognitive deficits limit their ability to work through the grief, the building of trust and the validation of their feelings are important by-products of therapy. The following case illustrates how psychotherapy with depressed, demented patients can help lead to successful resolution of grief and depression.

Ms. C.

Ms. C. was the youngest of three children. She was a star pupil and her father, a postmaster, encouraged her schooling. After graduating from high school, Ms. C. entered a teaching college and earned a certificate to teach history and Latin. Ms. C. was to remain a school teacher for 43 years. In her twenties, Ms. C. refused a marriage proposition so that she could care for her aging parents; in addition, Ms. C.'s older brother was mentally ill and required care at home. Ms. C.'s sister had a history of severe depression that ultimately led to suicide when she was in her sixties. Ms. C.'s brother and father died shortly thereafter. Ms. C. continued to care for her mother until the mother died in her nineties. In the same year, while in her sixties, Ms. C. retired from teaching.

She spent the next 20 years living alone on the family farm, and according to her nieces, she gradually became stubborn and eccentric. Early in her seventies, she had fallen and broken her hip. Later, she experienced a depressive episode. Ms. C. suffered a gradual onset of Alzheimer's disease beginning in her late seventies. Early cognitive declines included claiming to her niece that things were stolen. This occurred repeatedly, despite the fact that the niece always found the lost objects in Ms. C.'s house. Finally, when some of her cows died and she failed to have them removed, Ms. C. was brought to long-term care.

Ms. C.'s medical condition caused significant cognitive fluctuation. She had thorough neuropsychological assessments in September 1988 and January 1989, as well as screening assessments in August 1988 and December 1988. The results of these will be presented alongside of Ms. C.'s fluctuating medical condition. Upon admission (August 1988), Ms. C. was noted to have poor hearing and an acute confusional state. Wrist restraints and medication were used to subdue her. A neurology assessment found Ms. C. to be uncooperative and inattentive. One week later, however, it was discovered that Ms. C. had experienced a myocardial infarction.

She continued to suffer from medical complications, including a temperature of 102°, urinary tract infections, fecal impactions, and chronic constipation. Her level of alertness varied throughout the month; it was later discovered that she had suffered another myocardial infarction.

The first thorough neuropsychological assessment came at about that same time. Ms. C. was disoriented as to time and place. Deficiencies were noted in attention, verbal abstract reasoning, and memory. Verbal skills were determined to be less efficient than visuospatial ones.

Ms. C.'s medical condition stabilized between her first and second neuropsychological assessment. A three-and-a-quarter-pound weight gain was noted, leaving her underweight by seven pounds. She began gait training and was regularly using her walker. She refused to consider a hearing aid, however. On the second evaluation, performance on well-learned information was above average, but social judgment and abstract reasoning were below expectation and represented a decline. Verbal recall was above average, but some mild naming difficulties were present. Visuospatial abilities were severely impaired, as was non-verbal memory. It was concluded that verbal abilities were clearly a strength relative to visuospatial abilities. On the long-term-care unit, it was recommended that verbal instructions be used and that recreational activities be directed toward reading and conversation.

Ms. C.'s history revealed a high-functioning woman who was used to being self-sufficient and socially isolated. She had a progressing dementia that interfered with her ability to provide for her own care and, due to her declines in the past year, made her an unsuitable candidate for returning home. Neuropsychological reassessments following medical improvement revealed a woman with greater cognitive skills than were revealed on the first assessment, especially in areas of verbal functioning. Her ability to integrate facts and provide good judgments, however, was faulty. Ms. C.'s chief need was to adjust to her decline by grieving her loss of autonomy and health, yet her neuropsychological deficits interfered with her ability to do this.

One of the saddest aspects of providing psychological treatment to dementia patients is their experience of grief. Dementia patients clearly have intense grief, and they can be helped by supportive intervention, but only momentarily. Due to their cognitive limitations, they do not remember–nor can they integrate–their grieving episodes so that they can form some type of healing process. They often remain stuck in grief. The grief symptoms in the demented appear to be the same as those in normal elderly, but often any progress in successful grief is a very slow process. Ms. C. provided an example of some progress in her grieving. She was seen by the therapist twice a week, for 15-30 minutes each session. Early on, she believed that she could live alone and that her neighbors would help her. This was clearly an experience of denial. Two months later, she told the staff that she came into a lot of money and could now pay someone to take complete care of her at home. This reflected a form of bargaining. Although attempts were made to increase her pleasant events, she refused any such offerings. Later, she stated that if she could not return home she would die. Soon thereafter, depressive symptoms such as tearfulness and a new sober attitude were noted. Slowly, she began to enjoy reminiscing and reciting well-learned poetry. She was clearly healing some from her grief. Her talk about returning home subsided significantly. At this point, a number of pleasant events were added to her day: drawing, reading, reminiscing, and cooking. Her depression resolved, and she became very close to the staff.

Ms. C.'s case highlights important components of psychotherapy with demented patients. First, traditional supportive therapy can help to build trust and prepare the patient for a behavioral approach. Ms. C. was unable to increase her pleasurable activities until she trusted, and felt understood by, the therapist. By first allowing her to work through her feelings, she was later able to delight in the opportunities presented in long-term care.

GROUP PSYCHOTHERAPY

Group psychotherapy in long-term care has been the subject of many papers during the past 20 years. Burnside (1971) presented her group work that lasted two years. Her goals to facilitate communication among group members and to re-socialize withdrawn patients were put into action with a group of eight long-term-care patients. Following the two years of therapy, Burnside was struck by the pervasive themes of loss and the intensity of the group members' feelings. She also found the need for the group leader to be very active. Another early work focused on directives crucial to good group communication. These included giving patients full attention; asking for clarification when there is a misunderstanding; and respecting the ambivalence and anger caused by dependency.

Several authors in the last decade reviewed factors that are vital to effective group psychotherapy. Capuzzi, Gross, and Friel (1990) believed that withdrawal, isolation, and loneliness were the major problems in long-term-care patients. They identified four types of groups to help rectify these problems: (1) Reality Orientation Groups, which consist of daily 15- to 30-minute meetings to help those who are disoriented; (2) Remotivation Groups, which are four-week treatment programs consisting of 30- to 60-minute sessions per week; (3) Reminiscing Groups, where the group meets weekly to share memories; and (4) Psychotherapy Groups, which help with problems of depression, fear, anxiety, etc. Leszcz (1990) identified three types of psychotherapy groups. Psychodynamic Groups promote an increased sense of self, and the goal of therapy is to increase self-esteem. A Life Review Group can help restore feelings of worth and competence by tying together the past with the present. A Cognitive-Behavioral Group can help identify dysfunctional attitudes and distortions that worsen depression.

Abramson and Mendis (1990) focused on how to organize groups in long-term care. First, they stated, institutional commitment is necessary since extra efforts will be required by all staff. Second, the purpose and goals of the group should be determined prior to the first session. Examples included coping with loss, enhancing remaining skills, and increasing self-esteem. Third, they believe the therapy works best if there is interdisciplinary group leadership. This is important so that leaders complement one another by having different strengths. Finally, they stated that there should be consistency in scheduling groups and that there be no more than six group members per leader.

Other authors focused on the process involved in useful psychotherapy groups. Saul and Saul (1990) discussed joy as a powerful healing factor. Joys included relationships, achieving, helping, touching, learning, laughing, and simply living. Leszcz et al. (1985) believed that counteracting isolation was the major value of group therapy. Cooper (1984) also believed that groups helped to decrease loneliness created by loss. He noted that themes of loss and death were frequently mentioned in group. He also noted that the therapist was likely to encounter his or her own negative responses to aging. Therapists may fear a group member will die or be disgusted by the deterioration in old age; therapists may also feel powerless in responding to patient's neediness.

Parham et al. (1982) concluded that research demonstrated that group members improved, but that the no-treatment subjects did not. These researchers also concluded that no particular group treatment was more effective that any other. In fact, however, most studies have used very small samples and questionable methodology. Indeed, a number of recent studies have failed to find improvements in group members. Christopher et al. (1988) used the Community Competency Scale in pretesting eight older adults. The groups then met twice weekly for sessions on communication, social adjustment, and money management. At the posttest, there were no significant improvements. Hyer et al. (1987) studied cognitive-behavioral therapy with patients suffering from acute grief and those from post-traumatic stress disorder. Each group underwent 12 sessions. In a pre-posttest analysis, there were no post-group changes.

In studies that reported treatment improvement, the methodologies were weak. Lesser et al. (1981) reported on using reminiscence in a psychotic gero-psychiatric population. Six patients were seen in group for 22 weeks. Results indicated that problems decreased and positive behaviors increased, but raters were not blind. Ernst et al. (1978) gave group treatment for three months and used a pre-posttest design to measure cognition and affect. There were no significant changes.

REFOCUSING GROUP GOALS: PREVENTION OF EXCESS DISABILITY

Group psychotherapy is valuable in combating isolation and deterioration, but the goals of groups in long-term care must be changed. Too much focus has been placed on significantly improving cognition or on learning new psycho-social skills. Moderate-to-severely-impaired patients cannot often make these specific gains.

Group goals ought to focus on function. When talking about function, the concept of excess disability is a useful framework. Kahn (1965) was the first to define excess disability, and he defined it operationally. In motor tasks, for example, patients who did not perform any of their own activities of daily living tasks with the nursing assistants were asked in separate interviews to follow some commands (e.g., lift both legs, comb hair, get out of bed). The discrepancy between their performance with the interviewer and their behavior with the nursing assistants was termed "excess disability." In Kahn's original study, excess disability was found in 40% of long-term-care patients. Brody et al. (1971) furthered the work on excess disability. These authors defined excess disability as occurring when the patient's functional incapacity is greater than that warranted by the actual impairment. In their study, Brody and her colleagues hypothesized that through a highly individualized, multifaceted approach, excess disabilities could be reduced and positive change could be produced in patients. Over a one-year period, improved functioning was significantly greater in an experimental (versus a control) group of moderately-to-severely-demented patients. Recently, Lichtenberg (1990) focused on reducing psycho-social excess disabilities in geriatric long-term-care patients.

The stimulating interaction of a group, the rewarding relationship between therapist and patient, and the challenges presented during group discussions go a long way toward reducing excess disability. Goals for group members should, however, be individualized. Each group member has unique strengths and weaknesses. A case example will highlight this approach. Because there are many descriptions of group work with cognitively intact (Capuzzi, Gross, and Friel, 1990; Cooper, 1984; Leszcz, 1990; Steur et al., 1984) and with demented individuals (Ernst, 1978; and Fernie and Fernie, 1990), the present example will focus on groups with the mentally ill.

Group Case Example

Seven individual patients were targeted as high risk due to their propensity to isolate themselves or to be rebuffed by other patients and staff. The first patient, suffering from schizophrenia, was blind and becoming increasingly quiet and withdrawn. The second patient, suffering from schizophrenia as well, had stopped participating in recreational activities and was hallucinating more. The third and fourth patients, suffering from manic depression, were frequently engaging in verbal altercations with others and becoming increasingly paranoid. The fifth, sixth, and seventh patients suffered from major depression and were displaying reduced independence in their basic functional skills (i.e., ADLs). The idea of group therapy was presented to each patient individually. They were told that the group would be structured and would focus upon interacting with others.

The following topics were addressed in the 12-week, 45-minute group sessions: self-disclosure, self-esteem, loss, anger, assertiveness, empathy, and personal change (Lichtenberg, Heck, and Turner, 1988). Topics were introduced and defined through lecture and discussion, and were followed by experiential exercises designed to promote group sharing. For example, during the self-disclosure session, patients brought in magazine pictures that were meaningful to them.

The group process was one of enthusiasm and lively participation. Attendance was high (70% had perfect attendance), and as the sessions went by, the group discussions were more full and enriching. The "outcomes" for group members were not dramatic improvements, and it is unlikely that new "skills" were learned in the group and then practiced on the unit. The group's value was in helping prevent excess disability. Withdrawn patients became more active on a daily basis. Paranoid patients received regular feedback that they were valued; as a result, their delusions became less intense. Depressed patients continued to function and to improve their ADL skills. At the end of the sessions, the patients continued to want to meet. A less structured "stress management" group was implemented and met for three years.

The contention of this section was that group psychotherapy is valuable, but in nontraditional ways. The focus of most empirical studies on groups in long-term care has been to measure for improved cognition or specific psycho-social skills. The results have been consistently disappointing. The value of groups in long-term care was identified, however, by the early pioneers in this area (Burnside, 1971; Ernst et al., 1978): groups help prevent deterioration due to isolation.

SUMMARY

Therapeutic interventions and treatments have been an integral part of previous chapters, and they are directly related to the current discussion of psychotherapy. Neuropsychological assessment, for instance, was discussed in the context of translating the knowledge gained into practical, applicable treatments. The neuropsychological impressions and recommendations contribute to the therapist's understanding of the patient, so that psychotherapy can be tailored to the patient's strengths and weaknesses. For example, a psychotherapist working with a patient who has strong visuospatial skills but weak verbal skills may make use of illustrations or concrete items. Or, the therapist may even engage the patient in interactions with other patients or staff to learn the new behavior, rather than relying on traditional talk therapy to learn a behavior.

Psychotherapy, when used in conjunction with the therapist's involvement on an interdisciplinary team, can promote the therapeutic interactions between patient and staff. First, it gives the therapist a better understanding of the patient; the therapist can then help the team to understand and interact appropriately with the patient. Second, the therapist can directly promote the patient's more adaptive and reinforcing involvement with the staff. Although the numbers of long-term-care patients are usually so high that the psychologist cannot give the desired amount of time to each patient, Chapter 5 illustrated that the mental-health worker can be trained and given ongoing supervision to facilitate effective therapeutic interventions with patients. Therapy for alcohol-abusing elderly patients is effective in building a trusting relationship and in helping the patient reach sobriety. In addition, therapy can help the patient address the grief issues that are so often present in these patients. The therapist can also have a positive impact by dealing with sexuality and issues of intimacy, which are often ignored or avoided topics in the treatment of the elderly long-term-care patient.

REFERENCES

Abramson, T. and Mendis, K. (1990). The Organizational Logistics of Running a Dementia Group in a Skilled Nursing Facility. *Clinical Gerontologist, 9,* 111-122.

Barns, E.K., Sack, A., and Shore, H. (1973). Guidelines to Treatment Approaches: Modalities and Methods for Use with the Aged. *The Gerontologist, Winter,* 513-516.

Berger, K., and Zarit, S. (1978). Late Life Paranoid States: Assessment and Treatment. *American Journal of Orthopsychiatry, 48,* 528-537.

Brink, T.L. (1985). The Grieving Patient in Later Life. *Clinical Gerontologist, 4,* 117-127.

Brody, E., Kleban, M., and Silverman, H. (1971). Excess Disabilities of Mentally Impaired Aged: Impact of Individualized Treatment. *The Gerontologist, 11,* 124-133.

Burnside, I.M. (1971). Long-Term Group Work with Hospitalized Aged. *The Gerontologist, 11,* 213-218.

Butler, R.N. (1974). Successful Aging and the Role of the Life Review. *Journal of the American Geriatrics Society, 22,* 529-535.

Capuzzi, D., Gross, D., and Friel, S.E. (1990). Group Work with Elders. *Generations, Winter,* 43-48.

Christopher, F., Loeb, P., Zaretsky, H., and Jassani, A. (1988). A Group Psychotherapy Intervention to Promote the Functional Independence of Older Adults in a Long Term Rehabilitation Hospital: A Preliminary Study. *Clinical Gerontologist, 7,* 51-61.

Cooper, D.E. (1984). Group Psychotherapy with the Elderly: Dealing with Loss and Death. *American Journal of Psychotherapy, 38,* 203-215.

Ernst, P., Badash, D., Beran, B., Kosovsky, R., Lerner, K., and Kleinhauz, M. (1978). Sensory Stimulation of Elderly Patients. *Journal of the American Geriatrics Society, 26,* 315-326.

Fernie, B., and Fernie, G. (1990). Organizing Group Programs for Cognitively Impaired Elderly Residents of Nursing Homes. *Clinical Gerontologist, 9,* 123-134.

Goldfarb, A.I. (1952). Recommendations for Psychiatric Care in a Home for the Aged. *Journal of Gerontology, 8,* 343-347.

Hyer, L., Harrison, W.R., and Jacobsen, R.H. (1987). Later-Life Depression: Influences of Irrational Thinking and Cognitive Impairment. *Journal of Rational-Emotive Therapy, 5,* 43-49.

Kahn, R.L. (1965). Excess Disability in the Aged. *The Gerontologist, 4,* 328-329.

Knight, B. (1985). *Psychotherapy with Older Adults.* Sage Press: New York.

Langer, E., and Rodin, J. (1976). The Effects of Choice and Enhanced Personal Responsibility for the Aged: A Field Experiment in an Institutional Setting. *Journal of Personality and Social Psychology, 34,* 191-198.

Lawton, M.P., and Gottesman, L.E. (1974). Psychological Services to the Elderly. *American Psychologist, September,* 689-693.

Lesser, J., Lazarus, L.W., Frankel, R., and Havasy, S. (1981). Reminiscence Group Therapy with Psychotic Geriatric Inpatients. *The Gerontologist, 21,* 291-296.

Leszcz, M. (1990). Toward an Integrated Model of Group Psychotherapy with the Elderly. *International Journal of Group Psychotherapy, 40,* 379-399.

Lichtenberg, P.A. (1990). Reducing Excess Disabilities in Geropsychiatric Inpatients: A Focus on Behavioral Problems. *Clinical Gerontologist, 9*, 65-76.

Lichtenberg, P., Heck, G., and Turner, A. (1988). Medical Psychotherapy with Elderly Psychiatric Inpatients: Uses of Paraprofessionals in Treatment. *Medical Psychotherapy, 1*, 87-93.

Mintz, J., Steuer, J., and Jarvik, L. (1981). Psychotherapy with Depressed Elderly Patients: Research Considerations. *Journal of Consulting and Clinical Psychology, 49*, 542-548.

Parham, I.A., Priddy, J.M., McGovern, T.V., and Richman, C.M. (1982). Group Psychotherapy with the Elderly: Problems and Prospects. *Psychotherapy: Theory, Research and Practice, 19*, 437-443.

Rubin, R. (1977). Learning to Overcome Reluctance for Psychotherapy with the Elderly. *Journal of Geriatric Psychiatry, 10*, 215-227.

Saul, S., and Saul, S.R. (1990). The Application of Joy in Group Psychotherapy for the Elderly. *International Journal of Group Psychotherapy, 40*, 353-363.

Schulz, R. (1976). Effects of Control and Predictability on the Physical and Psychological Well-Being of the Institutionalized Aged. *Journal of Personality and Social Psychology, 33*, 563-573.

Sparacino, J. (1979). Individual Psychotherapy with the Aged: A Selective Review. *International Journal of Aging and Human Development, 9*, 197-221.

Teri, L., and Gallagher-Thompson, D. (1991). Cognitive-Behavioral Interventions for Treatment of Depression in Alzheimer's Patients. *The Gerontologist, 31*, 413-416.

Teri, L., and Lewinsohn, P. (1986). *Geropsychological Assessment and Treatment: Selected Topics.* Springer Publishing: New York.

Teri, L., and Logsdon, R. (1991). Identifying Pleasant Activities for Alzheimer Disease Patients: The Pleasant Events Schedule. *The Gerontologist, 31*, 124-127.

Thompson, L.W., Davies, R., Gallagher, D., and Krantz, S.E. (1986).Cognitive Therapy with Older Adults. *Clinical Gerontologist, 5*, 245-278.

Whitbourne, S. (1989). Psychological Treatment of the Aging Individual. *Journal of Integrative and Eclectic Psychotherapy, 8*, 161-173.

Williams, F.R. (1989). Bereavement and the Elderly: The Role of the Psychotherapist. *Clinical Gerontologist, 8*, 225-241.

Yesavage, J.A., and Karasu, T.B. (1982). Psychotherapy with Elderly Patients. *American Journal of Psychotherapy, 36*, 41-54.

Chapter 9

Adult Family Caregivers:
Stages of Caregiving
and Their Effect on Long-Term Care

Elderly patients receive expert physical and mental-health care while in a long-term-care facility, but family caregivers often go ignored. The literature on family caregiving to our nation's elderly citizens has become a major focus in clinical and social gerontology. Much of this information, however, has not made its way into the hands of long-term-care staff. This chapter will first focus on four major topics in caregiving: (1) the experience of adult children versus special caregivers; (2) gender effects on caregiving; (3) negative affect in caregivers; and (4) the physical health of caregivers. This will be followed by an in-depth description of caregiving stages. A stage model of caregiving has not been presented in the literature. Too often, caregiving is viewed through a cross-sectional analysis. Caregiving stages force one to think about this issue as a longitudinal, dynamic process and not as a static one. Case examples will be used to illustrate each caregiving stage. Case examples will also highlight the role of long-term-care staff in helping the family caregivers.

ADULT CHILDREN

Caring for an elderly parent has become so common that it is viewed as a normative experience (Brody, 1981; Lang and Brody, 1983; Brody, 1985). Researchers have dubbed this period as a "filial crisis" (Horowitz, 1985) or as a time for "filial maturity" (Brody, 1985). The crisis is represented in adult children struggling to realize and to accept that the aging parent is no longer the pillar of strength from the past. Four categories of caregiving were identified by Horowitz (1985) and were labeled "emotional support," "direct service provision," "mediation with formal organizations," and "financial assistance." Horowitz cited research that indicated it is the personal-care tasks, such as bathing and dressing, that are the most stressful aspect of caregiving for an adult child. Filial Maturity was presented by Brody as a developmental stage wherein adult children learn to meet their parents' dependency needs. Three major findings emerged from Brody's line of research. First, most adult child caregivers are women (daughters or daughters in-law). Second, many of these caregivers are caught in the middle between care needs of their own children and those of a parent. Last, many women have cared for several family members over the course of their lifetime.

Lang and Brody (1983) studied 161 women "caught in the middle" to learn more about the caregiving role adult children play. They found a wide variation, with 38% of the elderly mothers needing no help at all. Over one-fifth of the elderly parents needed their daughters to help with food shopping, and only 17% needed help with cooking, laundry, and housework. Finally, 22% required intensive care. Overall, the caregiving daughters averaged helping their mothers nine hours weekly. Living arrangement, however, was the major determinant of the amount of care provided. Those living with their elderly parent provided far more care than those living in separate dwellings.

Brody (1985) described the sacrifices many adult daughters made to be caregivers: twenty-eight percent had quit their job due to the elderly mother's need for care. Interestingly, many of these daughters had had "caregiving careers." One-half had helped an elderly father and one-third had helped other elderly relatives before helping their mothers. Despite all the time and energy they gave to their mothers, 60% reported feeling guilty about not being able to do more.

SPOUSAL CAREGIVERS

The major focus on adult caregivers has overwhelmingly been with adult children, particularly daughters. Spousal caregivers, however, make up the largest group of caregivers and may well experience the greatest problems. Over a decade ago, Fengler and Goodrich (1979) aptly named wives who were elderly and were caring for their husbands as "hidden patients." In a landmark study that examined the experiences of adult children and spousal caregivers, Cantor (1983) found that spousal caregivers had poorer health and experienced greater strain than did adult children. Based on her findings, Cantor concluded that while spousal caregivers were at greater risk than adult children, they were also the most neglected group of caregivers.

Other studies have provided support for Cantor's conclusions. One large study reported that spousal caregivers provided more assistance to the care receiver than did adult children (Soldo and Myllyluoma, 1983). Recently, Pruchno (1990) found that not only did spouses provide the most extensive and comprehensive care, but they also received minimal help from other sources.

NEGATIVE AFFECT

The single most studied aspect of caregivers has been negative affect, primarily in the form of depression and burden. Research on depression will be focused on here (for a complete review, see Schulz, Visintainer, and Williamson, 1990). The research has produced amazingly consistent results. It was originally hypothesized that caregivers who were caring for demented elders would have a higher rate of depression than those caring for an elder whose primary limitations were physical. Researchers found, however, that no matter what the care recipient's physical condition, there were no differences in the level of depression between caregiver groups.

Caregivers evidenced significantly higher rates of depression than did control subjects (Coppel et al., 1985; Haley et al., 1987; Gallagher et al., 1989; Lichtenberg and Barth, 1989; Morycz, 1985; and Schulz, Visintainer, and Williamson, 1990). These assessment studies have demonstrated that depression rates in caregivers range from 40%-50%. These findings are amazingly consistent, given that different methodologies were used. Coppel et al. (1985) and Gallagher et al. (1989) utilized the Research Diagnostic Criteria for Depression from the Schedule for Affective and Schizophrenic Disorders. Haley et al. (1987), Lichtenberg and Barth (1989), and

Morycz (1985) used self-report measures. Only Haley and his colleagues utilized a matched control group, and only Lichtenberg and Barth reported longitudinal data. Large-scale epidemiological studies of community-dwelling elderly have found the rate of major depression to be 2% and 19%, respectively (Blazer, Hughes, and George, 1987; Kramer et al., 1985). Clearly, caregiver depression far exceeds this. The role of depression in caregivers is often central to long-term-care placement. (This issue will be discussed again later.)

Recent studies have found new morbidity factors associated with depression. Lichtenberg, Manning, and Turkheimer (1993, in press) found minor depression in spousal caregivers to be associated with memory dysfunction in the caregivers themselves. Another study found caregiver depression to be related to the risk of physical abuse from the care recipient (Joslin et al., 1991).

One causal theory of depression in caregivers has received empirical support and led to practical interventions (Lichtenberg and Barth, 1990; Lovett and Gallagher, 1988). In Lewinsohn's social learning model of depression (1986), the relationship between low levels of pleasant activities, high levels of unpleasant activities, and the development of depression is emphasized. In the Lichtenberg and Barth (1990) study, for example, both daily stressors ($r = 0.63$) and pleasant activities ($r = 0.50$) were significantly related to depression scores, providing support for Lewinsohn's theory. Utilizing this theory, Lovett and Gallagher (1988) found that a ten-week problem-solving group helped to reduce depression in caregivers, while a supportive control group showed no such reduction.

GENDER ISSUES

Gender issues in caregiving are often overlooked. Researchers, however, have found important and somewhat unexpected differences between men and women who are spousal caregivers. It is women, ironically, that suffer more negative consequences than men. Studies from several different research centers have provided this converging evidence (Barusch and Spaid, 1989; Fitting et al., 1986; Pruchno and Resch, 1989; Zarit, Todd, and Zarit, 1986).

Barusch and Spaid (1989) found that in 121 caregivers, wives reported increased burden and depression when compared with husbands. Husbands were also more likely to receive home nursing and home-aid help. Male caregivers were significantly older than the women. Fitting et al. (1986) found the same results in a sample of 54 caregivers: husband caregivers were older and experienced less depression than did wife caregivers. In their longitudinal study of 64 caregivers, Zarit, Todd, and Zarit (1986) found women caregivers to have increased burden when compared with men caregivers. In this sample, men caregivers, on average, were nine years older than the women.

Pruchno and Resch (1989) were the researchers to directly assess the effects of age on burden. In their sample of 214 wives and 101 husbands, husbands were significantly older, and age was significantly related to burden (a reverse relationship). In this study, women were again more depressed than men and were less likely to receive additional assistance in caregiving than men.

Women caregivers appear to be at the highest risk for negative caregiving consequences. Two major reasons may explain this. First, since they receive less outside help than do husbands, wives provide more actual care. Second, wives are often younger when they become full-time caregivers. In each of the studies cited above, wives were in their low to mid sixties. In our society, this is generally a time for couples to enjoy a freedom from the responsibilities of childrearing and employment and to do the things they had yet to pursue (travel, hobbies, etc).

It is known that "off time" events such as premature illness and caregiving are associated with greater negative consequences (such as burden and depression) than are the more predictable "on time" events. As an older group, male caregivers, in comparison to women, may be more prepared for problems with health. This may, therefore, help them to adapt to the caregiving role more easily. Long-term-care staff must recognize that women caregivers may need considerable emotional support.

PHYSICAL HEALTH

Caregivers report poorer physical health than do control samples (Haley et al., 1987; Pruchno, 1990; Schulz, Visintainer, and Williamson, 1990). Health status has been measured in several ways, including self-reported general health, chronic conditions, psychotropic drug use, health-care utilization, and immunological markers. The results on health-care utilization were equivocal, with some studies finding increased utilization and others that did not (Gwyther and George, 1986; Haley et al., 1987; and Schulz, Visintainer, and Williamson, 1990).

Two areas of health, self-reported health and pychotropic drug use, have consistently been found to be worse in caregivers. Haley et al. (1987) found that, overall, caregivers' health status was poorer than was that for members of the control group. In addition, caregivers utilized physician services and psychotropic medications significantly more than did the control group. Similarly, Gwyther and George (1986) found psychotropic drug use was significantly higher among caregivers than control samples. Thus, caregivers were often self-medicating with medications prescribed for the care recipient. In the same study, health-care utilization and physician visits were not different between caregivers and controls.

The most unique study of physical health among caregivers was a comparison of helper T lymphocytes between caregivers and age-matched controls (Kiecolt-Glazer et al., 1987). Caregivers displayed significantly lower lymphocyte levels, which indicates poorer immune systems and increased risk for illness. In summary, although caregivers' physical health has not been studied to the extent of negative affect, the results indicate significantly poorer health for caregivers on a number of dimensions.

CAREGIVING STAGES

Caregiving is a dynamic, evolving process and not a static one. Each stage of caregiving brings its own unique challenges and problems. Due to its changing nature, long-term-care professionals need to be sensitive not only to general caregiving issues but also to the specific stages each caregiver experiences. Long-term-care staff will encounter family caregivers in a wide variety of situations. For example, a loved one may be temporarily staying in a long-term-care facility while recuperating from a stroke or broken hip. On the other hand, placement in long-term care may be permanent.

Stages of caregiving have not previously been proposed in the literature. Stages, however, can serve as useful guides in understanding an evolving experience such as caregiving. The stages should not be thought of rigidly, nor should rigid timeframes be affixed to each stage. Four stages of caregiving will be described:

1. *Detection:* Recognizing a need for caregiver support due to a decline in care-recipient functioning.
2. *Current Caregiving:* The period of time where a caregiver provides for the care recipient in the home.
3. *Transitional Caregiving:* The first year after placing the care recipient into long-term care.
4. *Post Caregiving:* The time after transitional caregiving, when the caregiver has had a chance to rebuild his or her life. This often includes the experience of bereavement, since care recipients typically die before the caregiver. Caregiving for a demented spouse will serve as the context for the following discussion of stages.

Stage 1: Detection

Recognizing the symptoms in the early stages of a dementia such as Alzheimer's disease is often very difficult. Indeed, it is striking to the extent that dementia patients retain their social skills and their basic language skills. They also retain the ability to converse appropriately and act politely. The symptoms of dementia are subtle, and the onset is gradual. As can be seen in Table 9.1, the major early symptoms of dementia include memory and personality changes. Chenoweth and Spencer (1986) reported on 289 caregivers, randomly selected, who were asked to describe the early dementing symptoms.

Sixty-two percent noticed memory loss and confusion. One-fifth noticed work-related problems and personality changes. Thirteen percent noticed specific problems related to driving. In 85% of cases, family members sought a medical consultation, with the dementia patient seeking medical help in only 15% of cases. Due to its subtle nature, detection of dementia can take months or years. This is a period of great anxiety and fear for the caregiver. Caregivers fear losing their loved one and react with denial. Denial, a normal

TABLE 9.1. Early Symptoms of Dementia

- Problems with recent memory
- Problems with confusion
- Patients seek to conceal deficits
- Patients become angry or withdrawn
- Patients refuse to seek medical help themselves

reaction to unwanted change, occurs when caregivers doubt their own eyes or do not catch on to symptoms of confusion and decline.

Stage 2: Current Caregiving

Caregiving to elder adults typically involves progressive neurological illnesses that often spur cognitive, behavioral, and personality changes in the care recipient. Common illnesses of care recipients include Alzheimer's disease, stroke, Parkinson's disease, heart disease, severe diabetes, and severe arthritis. Based on a number of studies, the following care-recipient problems are common and often worsen as the illness does (Barusch, 1988; Gilleard, Boyd, and Watt, 1982; Lichtenberg and Barth, 1989; and Rabins et al., 1982) (see Table 9.2).

The following are more detailed descriptions of several care recipient problems:

1. *Increased Dependency:* As care recipients become more impaired, their need for attention and care usually increases. This increasing dependency often leads them to want their caregiver nearby constantly. At times, care recipients may become upset whenever the caregiver attempts to leave the house without them. Indeed, as the care recipient's disease progresses, they are often unable to remain home alone for any length of time.

2. *Decreased Cognition:* Memory, mental flexibility, and problem-solving abilities often diminish drastically in patients with dementia. Thus, care recipients can lose their ability to accurately interpret everyday events and make sense of the world.

3. *Frustration/Catastrophic Reactions:* As care recipients lose their cognitive abilities and self-esteem, they become frightened. This fear is often expressed as anger and tantrum behavior. In 15%-30% of dementia cases, care recipients will become physically aggressive or verbally hostile (Barusch, 1988; Rabins et al., 1982). Care recipients may begin hiding things or become overtly suspicious of the caregiver, accusing them of trying to poison or kill them. Thus, in addition to the physical care they are providing, caregivers may also have to cope with daily accusations, anger, and the threat of physical violence.

4. *Nightwalking:* Physical and neurological illness in elderly care recipients often leads to dramatic changes in their sleeping cycle. Care recipients may begin to take frequent naps, leaving them awake during the night. Since the care recipient may require supervision at this time, caregivers must often forgo a good night's sleep. Moreover, disturbed sleep resulting from anxiety and concern in the care recipient can diminish the effects of obtained sleep.

5. *Incontinence:* Bowel and bladder incontinence is not only one of the most frustrating and upsetting problems in care recipients, but also one that can have severe health consequences. Skin breakdown due to incontinence and the development of sores are a significant concern. Incontinence, and its emotional consequences in caregivers, is a major factor in deciding to place a care recipient in long-term care. Chenoweth and Spencer (1986) reported that almost one-fifth of caregivers cited incontinence as a major determinant of long-term-care placement.

Caregiver Reactions

As the cognitive and physical status of a care recipient declines, there is a parallel process that happens to the caregivers (see Table 9.3). The circumstances under which care is provided plays a major role in contributing to these problems. In most cases, the current caregiver is a single, primary caregiver and is often receiving very little outside help (Pruchno, 1990). Caregivers typically bear the full responsibility and burden for all of the care recipient's needs for

TABLE 9.2. Common Problems in Care Recipients During Current Caregiving

- Increasing dependency
- Declining memory and other cognitive dysfunction
- Catastrophic reactions
- Night waking
- Hiding things
- Suspiciousness towards caregiver
- Becoming physically violent
- Communication problems
- Incontinence
- Increased irritability or apathy
- Impaired capacity for self-care

TABLE 9.3. Common Reactions of Caregivers During Current Caregiving

- Anger towards patient
- Guilt feelings
- Chronic fatigue
- Increasing depression
- Conflict with other family members
- Loss of friends
- Loss of hobbies
- Feelings of isolation
- Decline in physical health
- Agony over deciding how and when to place the patient in long term care
- Feeling bombarded by "helpful" suggestions from other relatives that did not help

a period of five to seven years. Suffice to say that it takes its toll. Caregivers reported common general difficulties to be such things as arguing with the care recipient; the care recipient not showing appreciation; missing the way the care recipient used to be; and worrying about becoming ill themselves (Barusch, 1988). Other common problems include:

1. *Depression, Anger, and Guilt:* Since depression was discussed earlier, anger and guilt will be focused on here. Care recipients—by becoming increasingly dependent and yet ungrateful or even suspicious, or by engaging in verbal or physical outbursts–produce normal frustration and anger in caregivers. Following these feelings of anger, however, caregivers feel guilty. The care recipients, after all, "cannot help themselves." Indeed it is a common phenomenon to find that caregivers, despite devoting themselves totally to their task, often feel that they are not doing enough (Brody, 1985).

2. *Conflict with Other Family Members:* Caregivers often feel hurt and angry that they receive so little help from other family members. In addition, family members are often overtly critical of caregivers, or give advice that is not helpful. A caregiver's sibling or adult child, for instance, may come from out of town to visit. After spending a pleasant and uneventful day with the care recipient, the relative may tell the caregiver that the caregiver has exaggerated the care recipient's impairment.

3. *Loss of Hobbies and Friends:* Caregiving removes the caregiver from an ability to enjoy leisure time or social activities. Indeed, many caregivers find that friends are unable to cope with the care recipient's declining mental and physical status. They may feel awkward, unaware of what to say or how to help. Or they may even be fearful of confronting their own mortality. Eventually, they withdraw, leaving the caregiver isolated and abandoned. Pagel, Erdly, and Becker (1987) found that even when contact is maintained with friends, the nature of the communication often becomes negative. This negative contact was significantly related to caregivers developing depression in a ten-month span.

4. *Chronic Fatigue:* Caregivers, by virtue of the care recipient's night waking and other behavioral problems, get too little rest and often become chronically fatigued. In addition, as mentioned earlier, caregivers fret over their own health and worry about becoming ill.

Current caregiving is an extremely stressful and busy time. Caregivers in this stage often do not get a chance to attend to their feelings of loss and grief. Indeed, they are too busy and too tired to concern themselves with their own reactions. Often, due to increased fatigue, depression, and the increasing physical care needs of the care recipient, current caregivers constantly worry about how long can they continue to provide care at home and when placement in long-term care will become necessary.

Intervention Strategies

Current caregivers need support and respite (see Table 9.4 for the various types of support and respite). Support is defined as a time of aid or help, and respite is defined as a time of relief. Many caregivers are unaware of their need for support or how to go about seeking it. They may also have concerns about being a burden on others and, thus, allow themselves too little respite. Caregivers must obtain physical and informational support in order to learn about the care recipient's illness and how to provide physical care. Caregivers may also obtain emotional and social support. Support groups or personal counseling can help with this. Caregivers need regular, two-to-four-hour respite breaks each week. Formal respite services for a nominal fee are common throughout the country. Informal respite can be arranged if caregivers know someone they can ask to stay with the care recipient. Hospitals and some long-term-care facilities provide longer respite services (1-14 days).

Caregivers must often be encouraged by others to get support and respite. Since caregivers typically place their own concerns secondary to the care recipient's, encouragement should stress the beneficial effect support and respite will have on the caregiving process. One effective way to do so is to link the very real possibility of a caregiver becoming disabled (due to poor health) if they do not regularly attend to their own needs. What follows is a case example of the Detection and Current Caregiving stages:

Mrs. G.

Mrs. G. was a homemaker in her late fifties when her husband, 15 years her senior, contracted Alzheimer's disease. For the first few years, no one recognized any of the symptoms. Mr. G. began to have problems at work. He was the director of a road department, and after several years on the job, began to be dissatisfied. He began fighting with his boss, who he was sure was out to harm him. After one year of almost constant turmoil, Mr. G. took a new, lower-paying job 100 miles away. In doing so, he forfeited most of his pension. In six months, he was fired from the new job for angry outbursts and general ineffectiveness. He could not find another job. One year later, the couple was running out of money. This time, Mrs. G. noticed that Mr. G. was confused and disoriented. A neurological workup concluded that he was suffering from probable Alzheimer's disease.

Mrs. G. was faced with the prospect of finding work and providing full-time care. She enrolled Mr. G. in a day-care program and found a secretarial position. Although she had two daughters in the area, she did not ask for, or allow, their help. Steadily, she became increasingly depressed. Her symptoms included insomnia, lack of energy, feeling depleted and hopeless, loss of appetite, and frequent crying spells. This went on for two years before she attended her first support-group meeting. She then entered personal counseling.

Mrs. G. was encouraged to seek support and respite from her children. They, as it turned out, were eager to help. Mrs. G. began to find some relief from her depression. Still, Mr. G.'s condition worsened, and he became unmanageable at home. He was eventually placed in a long-term-care facility.

Stage 3: Transitional Caregiving

The decision to place a loved one into a long-term-care facility is an agonizing one for caregivers. This section will provide an overview of the factors related to institutionalizing a care recipient; it will also describe the emotional experience of the caregivers. Research has consistently revealed that placing a care recipient in a long-term-care facility is related to both caregiver and care-recipient factors (Chenoweth and Spencer, 1986; Gwyther and George, 1986; Morycz, 1985; Stephens, Kinney, and Ogrocki, 1991; Zarit, Todd, and Zarit, 1986). The care recipient's state of confusion and increased need for physical care are significant predictors of long-term-care placement. Indeed, 72% of caregivers cited the overwhelming task of 24-hour care as a major reason for placement (Chenoweth and Spencer, 1986). One-fifth also cited care recipient problems, anger, and/or incontinence as major determinants of placement.

Three specific problems were most highly related to long-term-care placement. First, as mentioned earlier, many care recipients experience severe sleep disturbances. Since disturbed sleep cycles and night waking produce a need for constant supervision, caregivers can become exhausted to the point where their health declines.

TABLE 9.4. Types of Support and Respite

Support:	
•Physical	•Toileting, transferring patient
•Informational	•Learning the facts about dementia
•Emotional	•Sharing the pain with someone else
•Internal	•Coping strategies of individual
•Professional	•Individual or group treatment for depression
Respite:	
•Short Periods	•Respite "breaks" 2-4 hours each week
•Longer periods	•Overnight respite, one day-two weeks

Second, dangerous behaviors in care recipients–such as repeated episodes of aggression, severe wandering, or using appliances in a consistently dangerous fashion–also contribute to the decision for placement. Finally, incontinence, as mentioned before, is a problem that caregivers can find extremely difficult to accept and cope with.

The caregiver's mental health, particularly their perceived level of burden and strain (i.e., felt stress) is highly related to long-term-care placement. In one longitudinal study, covering two years, 34% of care recipients entered a long-term-care facility. Caregiver burden was more strongly associated with placement than was the severity of cognitive deficits (Zarit, Todd, and Zarit, 1986). In another study that compared 60 in-home caregivers with 60 caregivers whose spouses were in long-term care, Stephens, Kinney, and Ogrocki (1991) found placement to be highly related to caregiver strain. These findings underscore the importance of intervening with caregivers early on in caregiving and encouraging them to get needed support and respite.

Caregiver Adjustment

The transition the caregiver makes after placing a spouse in long-term care has been previously neglected, but it is a very dramatic one. Many long-term-care workers have assumed that the removal of the care recipient from the home leads to relief from stresses and strains for the caregiver. This does not, however, appear to be the case. In fact, dramatic grief reactions follow, often resulting in increased depression and decreased physical health (Greenfield, 1984; Lichtenberg and Barth, 1989; Townsend, Heiselman, and Deimling, 1989). Caregivers who, during current caregiving, were too busy and too tired to attend to their grief symptoms are now faced with these intense feelings. One longitudinal study found that two-thirds of transitional caregivers were reporting depression (Lichtenberg and Barth, 1989; see Table 9.5). Spousal caregivers, particularly, reported increased depression and decreased physical health subsequent to placement. Common caregiver reactions following long-term-care placement include the following:

1. *Guilt and Feelings of Failure:* Caregivers are conflicted by their desire to preserve and protect their family member while

trying to find a new caregiver arrangement (Greenfield, 1984). Caregivers wonder if they just "dumped" their loved one, and they often feel like failures for being unable to continue giving care at home.

2. *Loneliness:* Given that friends have drifted away and there has been little time for social activities, the separation, particularly for spouses, leaves caregivers feeling empty and lonely. After spending years attending to caregiving tasks and care recipient's needs, homes are overwhelmingly quiet and still. In one study, 90% of caregivers reported loneliness as a significant problem during this stage.

3. *Identity:* Caregivers–after spending most of their waking hours, day in and day out for several years, caring for their loved one–are faced with the task of building a new life and new identity. Often, their friends and hobbies have long been lost. Although frustrated by a full-time caregiving role, they fear giving it up.

Interventions to Help Transitional Caregivers

It has only been very recently that Morgan and Zimmerman (1990) examined ways to ease the caregiver transition to long-term care. They identified five categories that helped ease the transition for caregivers:

1. Emotional support (particularly approval from other family members) was identified as beneficial to caregivers.

2. Control of their situation was also identified by caregivers as being helpful. This included participating in their loved one's care and getting to know the long-term-care staff personally. In addition, it was important to caregivers that staff view them as the responsible party for decision making for their loved one.

3. Acceptability of the long-term-care facility was another important factor. Caregivers compared the long-term-care facility to their own home, their ideal long-term-care facility, and to other long-term-care facilities they had seen.

4. Acceptance of the situation was also an important element in the caregiver's transition. This included accepting that they

could no longer care for their loved one at home, as well as accepting the progressive nature of the care recipient's disease.

5. Finally, receiving permission to utilize a long-term-care facility (i.e., coming from family and/or a command from a physician that the long-term-care placement was necessary) was deemed helpful by caregivers.

Long-term-care staff can aid transitional caregivers by utilizing Lewinsohn's model of depression. Recall that decreased positive interactions and increased negative ones caused depression. By helping caregivers to experience positive visits with their loved one, and by gently encouraging caregivers to seek out positive experiences away from the facility, adjustment can by facilitated. The following case illustrates the emotional difficulties encountered in transitional caregiving.

Mr. W.

Mr. W.'s case highlights the powerful grief that is often experienced during the early post-caregiving stage. Mr. W., as a current caregiver, was too busy to attend to his losses. During early transitional caregiving, he was aware of his loneliness and the finality of his separation from his wife. He felt guilty for placing his wife in a nursing home. Although he remained physically healthy, he was experiencing increased minor physical complaints.

Mr. W. was a 72-year-old, retired machinist whose wife suffered from Alzheimer's disease and who had been cared for at home by Mr. W. for six years. For the last two years, he was an active member of the local Alzheimer's Support Group. During a three-month span, his wife's condition had deteriorated. She was resistive to ADL care, did not sleep at night, and was physically combative. Mr. W. received intensive help from home health care, his children, and a private caretaker during this decline. He had decided some months previously to apply for a long-term-care bed and anticipated moving his wife to the home when he could no longer care for her.

He summed up his life as a caregiver as "very stressful." Despite this, he remained active in the community, was in good health, financially satisfied, and reported few daily hassles. He used many

TABLE 9.5. Rate of Depression During Caregiving Strategies (Lichtenberg and Barth, 1989)

Current Caregiving	40-50%
Transitional Caregiving	60-65%
Post-Caregiving	10-20%

coping strategies. He received emotional support from his children, and both he and his wife still enjoyed listening to music. He also made good use of respite opportunities when the nursing help came in. On a scale of depression, he scored in the mentally healthy range. Physically, he reported some stomach problems, sinus difficulties, and a lack of energy. He was optimistic about his future and looked forward to getting more rest.

After five months, Mr. W. was clearly experiencing difficulty. He reported finding the adjustment to life after his wife's placement in the nursing home as "very difficult." He was depressed when visiting his wife in the nursing home, he was lonely, and he experienced deep sorrow over the ending of their life together. He felt guilty for not being able to keep his wife at home. During her first four months in the nursing home, Mrs. W. experienced two serious kidney infections, causing Mr. W .to prepare for her death. She was, however, medically stable at the time of our interview. Compared to the first interview, Mr. W. had cut back on his social activities, continued to report few hassles, and was financially secure. Mr. W. continued to report some depression. He now had frequent headaches, complaints of vague aches and pains, numbness, more difficulty reading, bothersome ringing in his ears, a lack of energy, anxiety, and some hopelessness.

Stage 4: Post-Caregiving

The final stage of caregiving occurs after the caregiver has had time to adjust to the long-term-care transition. Caregivers have often spent time resting and recuperating from the physical demands of caregiving. Although the emotional responsibilities of caregiving remain, only one-fifth of caregivers at this stage reported depression (see Table 9.5). During post-caregiving, caregivers must often experience the loss of their loved one to death.

Bass and Bowman (1990) studied the bereavement phenomenon. Specifically, they tested whether caregiving strain predicted more or less difficulty with bereavement. Their findings supported the hypothesis that the greater the caregiving strain, the greater was the bereavement strain. This finding is consistent with many studies of bereaved that show strongly ambivalent relationships produced far more difficult bereavement experiences than did more positive relationships.

A truly remarkable aspect of post-caregiving, however, is the caregivers' ability to make the most out of trying experiences, as well as their ability to continue to cherish life. For the most part, post-caregivers appear able to grieve successfully, to heal, and to lead a full life again. The following case example illustrates this rejuvenation.

Mrs. F.

Mrs. F.'s case is an example of a caregiver who was depressed in transitional caregiving and who improved during later post-caregiving. During this time, Mrs. F. was able to assume a new identity. By obtaining rest, social support, and reinvesting herself in a hobby, Mrs. F. was able to move away from the ruminating, tearful, and hopeless individual she was during transitional caregiving. She created a new way of life for herself, was increasingly more comfortable living alone, and was freed of depression.

Mrs. F. was a 74-year-old homemaker whose husband suffered from Alzheimer's disease and who had been cared for at home by Mrs. F. for five years. He was placed in long-term care due to his need for increased care, his combativeness, and his wandering. Mrs. F. had received almost no help with her husband's care, and she had never been a support-group member.

Mrs. F. found the transitional stage of caregiving "very difficult." Chief among her complaints was loneliness, separation, and worry over her husband's condition. Her physical health was fair—she suffered from rheumatic arthritis. Mrs. F. had almost no social outlets, but reported few hassles and was financially secure. However, she was moderately depressed. She was generally dissatisfied, had dropped activities and interests, ruminated about her husband, worried about her future, was often tearful, felt hopeless, and was devoid of energy. She also complained of poor appetite and disrupted sleep.

One year later, Mrs. F. reported that her husband's condition was basically stable, although he was "more forgetful." Her physical health remained fair. She continued to be financially secure, and she reported even fewer hassles; she also reported few activities. In contrast to the previous year, Mrs. F. said she was sleeping well, was now spending a good deal of her time baking, and was in close contact with a sister who was now being very supportive. On the GDS, Mrs. F. obtained a score of eight, indicating absence of depression. Compared to the first interview, she reported less apathy, more energy, less tearfulness, and less hopelessness. She no longer viewed her life as empty, and she was in good spirits most of the time.

REFERENCES

Barusch, A.S. (1988). Problems and Coping Strategies of Elderly Spouse Caregivers. *The Gerontologist, 28,* 677-685.

Barusch, A.S., and Spaid, W.M. (1989). Gender Differences in Caregiving: Why Do Wives Report Greater Burden? *The Gerontologist, 29,* 667-676.

Bass, D.M., and Bowman, K. (1990). The Transition from Caregiving to Bereavement: The Relationship of Care-Related Strain and Adjustment to Death. *The Gerontologist, 30,* 35-42.

Blazer, D., Hughes, D.C., and George, L.K. (1987). The Epidemiology of Depression in an Elderly Community Population. *The Gerontologist, 27,* 281-287.

Brody, E.M. (1981). "Women in the Middle" and Family Help to Older People. *The Gerontologist, 21,* 471-480.

Brody, E. (1985). Parent Care as a Normative Stress. *The Gerontologist, 25,* 19-29.

Cantor, M.H. (1983). Strain Among Caregivers: A Study of Experience in the United States. *The Gerontologist, 23,* 597-604.

Chenoweth, B., and Spencer, B. (1986). Dementia: The Experience of Family Caregivers. *The Gerontologist, 26,* 267-272.

Coppel, D.B., Burton, C., Becker, J., and Fiore, J. (1985). Relationships of Cognitions Associated with Coping Reactions to Depression in Spousal Caregivers of Alzheimer's Disease Patients. *Cognitive Therapy and Research, 9,* 253-266.

Fengler, A.P., and Goodrich, N. (1979). Wives of Elderly Disabled Men: The Hidden Patients. *The Gerontologist, 19,* 175-182.

Fitting, M., Rabins, P., Lucas, M.J., and Eastham, J. (1986). Caregivers for Dementia Patients: A Comparison of Husbands and Wives. *The Gerontologist*, 26, 248-252.

Gallagher, D., Rose, P., Rivera, P., Lovett, S., and Thompson, L. (1989). Prevalence of depression in family caregivers. *Gerontologist*, 29, 449-455.

Gilleard, C.J., Boyd, W.D., and Watt, G. (1982). Problems in Caring for the Elderly Mentally Infirm at Home. *Archives of Gerontology and Geriatrics*, 1, 151-158.

Greenfield, W.L. (1984). Disruption and Reintegration: Dealing with Familial Response to Nursing Home Placement. *Journal of Gerontological Social Work*, 8, 15-21.

Gwyther, L.P., and George, L.K. (1986). Symposium: Caregivers for Dementia Patients: Complex Determinants of Well-Being and Burden. *The Gerontologist*, 26, 245-247.

Haley, W.E., Levine, E.G., Brown, L., Berry, J.W., and Hughes, G.H. (1987). Psychological, Social, and Health Consequences of Caring for a Relative with Senile Dementia. *Journal of the American Geriatrics Society*, 35, 405-411.

Horowitz, A. (1985). Family Caregiving to the Frail Elderly. In *Annual Review of Gerontology and Geriatrics*. Vol. 5 (C. Eisdorfer, M.P. Lawton, and G.L. Maddox, editors), 194-246. Springer Publishing Co.: New York.

Joslin, B.L., Coyne, A.C., Johnson, T.W., Berbig, L.J., and Potenza, M. (1991). Dementia and Elder Abuse: Are Caregivers Victims or Villains? Annual Scientific Meeting of the Gerontological Society of America. November: San Francisco.

Kiecolt-Glaser, J.K., Glaser, R., Shuttleworth, E.C., Dyer, C.S., Ogrocki, P., and Speicher, C.E. (1987). Chronic Stress and Immunity in Family Caregivers of Alzheimer's Disease Victims. *Psychosomatic Medicine*, 49, 523-535.

Kramer, M., German, P.S., Anthony, J.C., Von Korff, M., and Skinner, E.A. (1985). Patterns of Mental Disorders among the Elderly Residents of Eastern Baltimore. *Journal of the American Geriatrics Society*, 33, 236-245.

Lang, A.M. and Brody, E.M. (1983). Characteristics of Middle-aged Daughters and Help to Their Elderly Mothers. *Journal of Marriage and the Family*, 45, 193-202.

Lewinsohn, P., Munoz, R., Youngren, M., and Zeiss, A. (1986). *Control Your Depression*. Prentice Hall: New York.

Lichtenberg, P.A., and Barth, J.T. (1989). The Dynamic Process of Caregiving in Elderly Spouses: A Look at Longitudinal Case Reports. *Clinical Gerontologist*, 9, 31-44.

Lichtenberg, P.A., and Barth, J.T. (1990). Depression in Elderly Caregivers: A Longitudinal Study to Test Lewinsohn's Model of Depression. *Medical Psychotherapy*, 3, 147-156.

Lichtenberg, P.A., Manning, C.A., and Turkheimer, E. (1993). In Press, Vol. 12. Memory Dysfunction in Depressed Spousal Caregivers.

Lovett, S., and Gallagher, D. (1988). Psychoeducational Interventions for Family Caregivers. *Behavior Therapy*, 19, 321-330.

Morgan, A., and Zimmerman, M. (1990). Easing the Transition to Nursing Homes: Identifying the Needs of Spousal Caregivers at the Time of Institutionalization. *Clinical Gerontologist, 9*, 1-17.

Morycz, R.K. (1985). Caregiving Strain and the Desire to Institutionalize Family Members with Alzheimer's Disease. *Research on Aging, 3*, 329-361.

Pagel, M.D., Erdly, W.W., and Becker, J. (1987). Social Networks: We Get By with (and in Spite of) a Little Help from Our Friends. *Journal of Personality and Social Psychology, 53*, 793-804.

Pagel, M., Becker, J., and Coppel, D. (1985). Loss of Control, Self-Blame, and Depression: An Investigation of Spouse Caregivers of Alzheimers Patients. *Journal of Abnormal Psychology, 94*, 169-182.

Paris-Stephens, M.A., Kinney, J.M., and Ogrocki, P.K. (1991). Stressors and Well-Being Among Caregivers to Older Adults with Dementia: The In-Home Versus Nursing Home Experience. *The Gerontologist, 2*, 217-223.

Pruchno, R.A. (1990). The Effects of Help Patterns on the Mental Health of Spouse Caregivers. *Research on Aging, 12*, 57-71.

Pruchno, R.A., and Resch, N.L. (1989). Husbands and Wives as Caregivers: Antecedents of Depression and Burden. *The Gerontologist, 29*, 159-165.

Rabins, P.V., Mace, N.L., and Lucas, M.J. (1982). The Impact of Dementia on the Family. *Journal of the American Medical Association, 248*, 333-335.

Schulz, R., Visintainer, P., and Williamson, G.M. (1990). Psychiatric and Physical Morbidity Effects of Caregiving. *Journal of Gerontology: Psychological Science, 45*, 181-191.

Soldo, B.J., and Myllyluoma, J. (1983). Caregivers Who Live with Dependent Elderly. *The Gerontologist, 23*, 605-611.

Stephens, M., Kinney, J., and Ogrocki, P. (1991). Stressors and Well-being Among Caregivers to Older Adults with Dementia: The In-Home Versus Nursing Home Experience. *The Gerontologist, 31*, 217-223.

Townsend, A.L., Heiselman, T., and Deimling, G.T. (1989). Impact of Nursing Home Care on Family Members' Stress and Mental Health. Annual Scientific Meeting of Gerontological Society of America. November: Minneapolis.

Zarit, S.H., Todd, P.A., and Zarit, J.M. (1986). Subjective Burden of Husbands and Wives as Caregivers: A Longitudinal Study. *The Gerontologist, 26*, 260-266.

Index

31,062

X95